THIS JOURNAL
BELONGS TO:

....
....

STERLING
New York

An Imprint of Sterling Publishing Co., Inc.
122 Fifth Avenue
New York, NY 10011

STERLING and the distinctive Sterling logo
are registered trademarks of Sterling Publishing Co., Inc.

ISBN: 978-1-4549-4205-4

Distributed in Canada by Sterling Publishing Co., Inc.
c/o Canadian Manda Group, 664 Annette Street
Toronto, Ontario M6S 2C8, Canada
Distributed in the United Kingdom by GMC Distribution Services
Castle Place, 166 High Street, Lewes, East Sussex BN7 1XU, England
Distributed in Australia by NewSouth Books
University of New South Wales, Sydney, NSW 2052, Australia

For information about custom editions, special sales, and premium
and corporate purchases, please contact Sterling Special Sales
at 800-805-5489 or specialsales@sterlingpublishing.com.

Manufactured in India

2 4 6 8 10 9 7 5 3 1

sterlingpublishing.com

Interior design by Christine Heun
Cover design by Elizabeth Mihaltse Lindy
Image Credits Cover: perori/Shutterstock.com;
Interior: Icons from Getty Images: Digital Vision Vectors: artvea (tulip);
ulimi (sun); -VICTOR- (hearts); iStock/Getty Images Plus: Fatma sari
(lotus); Olga Prokopeva (prayer hands)

INTRODUCTION

Life has a way of throwing us curveballs. The promotion you wanted may be given to someone else. That rock-solid relationship you thought would last forever may stall out or disappear unexpectedly. A family member or friend may pass away. A critical illness could appear just as you've made positive changes for your health. Or you may experience a financial hardship you never thought could happen to you.

Whatever challenges and hardships you may face, it is important to develop skills to help you overcome adversity and become a more resilient person who can get through difficulties and bounce back. Every human being has the capacity to be resilient. It is part of who we all are; it's built into our DNA to survive. However, at times we find ourselves reaching for tools, reassurances, inspirations, or connections to help us traverse the most difficult moments.

Incorporating the latest psychology and neuroscience research, this journal will provide you with science-based tools—as well as inspirational quotes, stories, and writing prompts—to strengthen your resilience. It will help you establish new behaviors, embrace positive thoughts, and be proactive. It will bring you closer to developing habits that will assist you in navigating life challenges and become stronger from them. Dare I say the work in this journal will help you become more "bounce back-able."

As you journal, you might feel like you're doing the same types of exercises over and over. That's by design: ten specific resilience traits are woven throughout these pages. You will also notice that there are some themes subtly rotating within four-week cycles. These have been strategically planned out to reinforce key areas of growth as follows: setting priorities (prioritizing happiness and/or making commitments to yourself); offering kindness to others, both anonymously or openly, as well as being kind to yourself; exploring the concepts of acceptance and the power of forgiveness; and establishing a practice of deliberately expressing gratitude, appreciating others, and regularly acknowledging yourself.

We're trying to create new, healthier habits—ones shown to boost resilience—through repetition. And who knows? As you get to later entries, you might even have a fresher take on an earlier prompt.

Allow these five-minute journaling prompts to be the start of your journey toward a happier future. This time is just for you. Enjoy it!

Making a Distinction According to researcher Dr. Jonathan R. H. Tudge, in defining gratitude there are two schools of thought:

- *Gratitude as a positive emotion—being grateful for the nice things that happen.*

- *Gratitude as a virtue—being grateful to those who have helped us. Ideally, reciprocity is part of the process, too.*

Today Write about the definition that resonates more for you and why.

_____

_____

_____

_____

_____

_____

_____

_____

_____

_____

Defining Gratitude #1 Robert A. Emmons, PhD, arguably the world's leading scientific expert on gratitude, contends that gratitude has two components. The first is an affirmation of goodness. Gratitude reinforces the notion that the world is a good place, and that we've been the recipients of its gifts and benefits.

Today Reflect on your life in recent days. Make a short list of affirmations of goodness you've experienced in your own life and that of others. Two or three examples of each are sufficient.

_____

_____

_____

_____

_____

_____

_____

_____

_____

_____

_____

Defining Gratitude #2 The second component of Dr. Emmons's definition of gratitude is figuring out for yourself where gratitude originates. Where does it come from? Does it originate in a higher power? Could a positive reflection of ourselves create the experience?

Today Write about what or who may be the origin of your gratitude. This is completely personal, so write from your heart.

_____

_____

_____

_____

_____

_____

_____

_____

_____

_____

_____

The Magic of Three Martin Seligman, PhD, commonly known as the founder of Positive Psychology, suggests that using the "Three Good Things" method increases happiness by training your brain to notice the good things that have happened during the day:

1. Every day, either in the morning or just before bed, reflect on your day.

2. Then think of three things that went well.

3. Write them down. Meditate on them for a few moments.

Today Write three good things that happened to you today at work/at school/at an event.

_____

_____

_____

_____

_____

_____

_____

_____

_____

Evolutionary DNA Researchers believe that gratitude is deeply rooted in our DNA (the molecule that contains our genetic code) and our exposure to modeling during early childhood development. In their studies, they observed that the desire to repay generosity can be expressed as gratitude. Such reciprocity creates social bonds, such as friendship, and a community of allies and helpful people.

Today Write about how gratitude was modeled or directly taught to you. How have these lessons helped you form stronger bonds with others?

_____

_____

_____

_____

_____

_____

_____

_____

_____

_____

Four-Step Cycle of Gratitude The Developing Gratitude Research Group, comprised of researchers from the United States and Brazil, details gratitude as a four-step cycle, for example:

1. Sally does something nice for Nancy.

2. Nancy feels good about what Sally did.

3. Nancy recognizes the intention and value of Sally's gesture or gift.

4. Nancy is motivated to reciprocate.

Nancy may directly thank Sally. It is also possible that Nancy will pass a kindness onto another person.

Today Write about a kindness that was given to you, and was explained as follows: "Someone helped me when I needed it, so I'm passing that same kindness onto you."

_____

_____

_____

_____

_____

_____

_____

It Is Love The social bonds that gratitude creates are a form of love, states Dr. Emmons. That love is the feeling of being cared for or supported by another person.

Today Write about your own experience of feeling loved and cared for by another person in this context.

_____

_____

_____

_____

_____

_____

_____

_____

_____

_____

_____

_____

Another Take on Gratitude University of California–Berkeley researcher Summer Allen narrows gratitude down to three concise categories:

1. **Affect Trait:** An overall tendency to be a grateful person.
2. **Mood:** Levels of gratitude fluctuating throughout the day.
3. **Emotional:** A fleeting feeling, based on receiving something positive.

Today Write about the category of gratitude the people surrounding you fall into. Where do you fit into these categories?

_____

_____

_____

_____

_____

_____

_____

_____

_____

Organizing Principle The interconnectivity of gratitude makes it an organizing principle of life itself, suggests psychologist Robert Emmons. He states, "Gratitude is the truest approach to life. We did not create or fashion ourselves. We did not birth ourselves. Life is about giving, receiving, and repaying. We are receptive beings, dependent on the help of others, on their gifts and their kindness."

Today Write about your level of comfort with the concept of being dependent on others.

_____

_____

_____

_____

_____

_____

_____

_____

_____

_____

_____

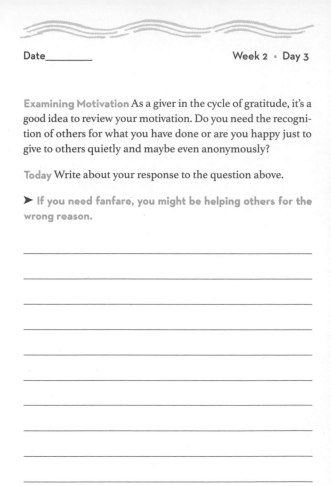

Examining Motivation As a giver in the cycle of gratitude, it's a good idea to review your motivation. Do you need the recognition of others for what you have done or are you happy just to give to others quietly and maybe even anonymously?

Today Write about your response to the question above.

➤ If you need fanfare, you might be helping others for the wrong reason.

_____

_____

_____

_____

_____

_____

_____

_____

_____

_____

_____

The Prefrontal Cortex University of Southern California neuroscience researcher Glenn Fox, PhD, identified the medial prefrontal cortex as the region of the brain that is stimulated during moments of gratitude. This is the area where the two hemispheres of the brain meet—an area that is also associated with feelings of empathy and relief, and where processing other people's perspective is thought to originate.

Today Write about a moment of gratitude you have experienced recently that filled you with relief, empathy, or an appreciation of another person's perspective.

_____

_____

_____

_____

_____

_____

_____

_____

_____

_____

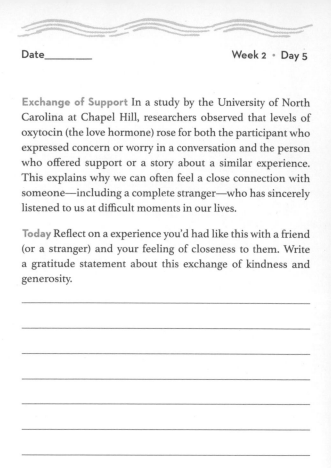

Exchange of Support In a study by the University of North Carolina at Chapel Hill, researchers observed that levels of oxytocin (the love hormone) rose for both the participant who expressed concern or worry in a conversation and the person who offered support or a story about a similar experience. This explains why we can often feel a close connection with someone—including a complete stranger—who has sincerely listened to us at difficult moments in our lives.

Today Reflect on a experience you'd had like this with a friend (or a stranger) and your feeling of closeness to them. Write a gratitude statement about this exchange of kindness and generosity.

_____

_____

_____

_____

_____

_____

_____

_____

_____

_____

Distract and Deflect Anne Wilson Schaef, a psychotherapist and the author of *When Society Becomes an Addict,* points out that in our fast-paced world of 80-hour workweeks, we also tend to get distracted by social media. These distractions deflect our attention and keep us from noticing the struggles of others who are close by, as well as others around the world. Schaef describes distraction and deflection as addictive behaviors that prevent us from being engaged with one another.

Today Write about a part of your day that you carve out, specifically, to tune into others around you. In that place, what insights have you gained?

_____

_____

_____

_____

_____

_____

_____

_____

Doing, Being, and Having Clinical psychologist and author Paul W. Pruyser offers us a multilevel definition of *gratitude*. *Gratia,* the Latin word most associated with gratitude, also means grace, graciousness, and gratefulness. So the root word for *gratitude* refers to kindness, generosity, gifts, and the act of giving and receiving.

Today Write about the element of Pruyser's definition that you'd like to experience more of in this process.

_____

_____

_____

_____

_____

_____

_____

_____

_____

_____

_____

_____

The Power of Being According to Paul Pruyser's definition of gratitude, there is an important aspect of gratitude that is overlooked: the ability to be kind, to be gracious, and to be grateful. These are states of being. Every month I will ask you to set an intention for the coming weeks. This will be an exercise in awakening your awareness as to how you want to be present in the world and with others.

Today Write about your intention for how you want to be in the world for the next few weeks. What do you desire to be that will create a more well-rounded gratitude state? Write it in a statement following this prompt: *My intention is to be XYZ.*

➤ Some ideas could be to be more patient, kind, aware of others, or appreciative of a particular person or group.

_____

_____

_____

_____

_____

_____

_____

_____

Handshake Today, allow yourself to embody gratitude for any person you meet. Be humble, be kind, be generous, and express your appreciation for them. Words are fine but try to feel all these things, as you offer another person a handshake or—in Covid-19 times—an elbow bump.

Today Write about what gratitude actually feels like to you, in your own body. That's exactly the state you're looking to convey to others without words.

_____

_____

_____

_____

_____

_____

_____

_____

_____

_____

_____

Quiet as a Mouse As I toiled away for hours writing my last book, my sweet husband would gently open my office door, place a cup of tea or something to eat on my desk, and then softly close the door again. I often think about his smiling face and his kindness; it fills my heart with gratitude that he supports the work that I love to do.

Today Write about a time when a cup of tea or a gentle act of support touched your heart.

_____

_____

_____

_____

_____

_____

_____

_____

_____

_____

Something Other Than Ourselves Universally, religions as diverse as Christianity, Hinduism, and Wicca teach prayer as a way to express thankfulness. This is a reflection of the belief that the goodness that comes to each of us arrives from a source outside of ourselves.

Today Write your own personal prayer, meditation, or visualization that expresses gratitude to your Source.

➤ The Source—a belief system that makes sense to you—can be as individual as you are.

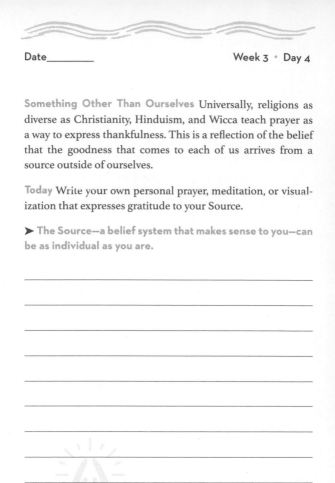

_____

_____

_____

_____

_____

_____

_____

_____

_____

_____

_____

Seeking Agency Human beings desire to see *agency* in the world. That is to say, they seek out the origin of the benevolence, grace, and kindness around them, according to psychologist Michael McCullough of the University of Miami.

Today Consider your most recent experience of having something wonderful happen in your life. Write about your reaction to that experience. Did you wonder about or actively try to find out where it came from?

_____

_____

_____

_____

_____

_____

_____

_____

_____

_____

_____

_____

Casting a Spotlight The gratitude cycle is based on giving and receiving. In different cultures, the visibility of indebtedness varies widely, so there is no one right answer to the following questions: Would you be hurt or resentful if someone didn't thank you for a kindness or favor? Why would you feel that way?

Today Write your answer to the above questions and explain the factors that influenced your response.

➤ **Ask a friend the same questions. You might gain some really amazing insights from their answers.**

In Translation In the Burmese language, Pali, the word *kataññu* means to remember what has been done; remembrance serves as a pathway to gratitude. Without acknowledgment that in some way another has helped or given something valuable to us, there is no basis to express thanks. *Kataññu* is a key aspect of gratitude that connects us to one another and builds interconnectedness.

Today Write about someone who has given you some form of assistance, and who you've forgotten to thank.

➤ Remember that being mindful is most important here, even if you cannot deliver your message of thanks today.

_____

_____

_____

_____

_____

_____

_____

_____

_____

The Secret to Life In a 2017 Pew Research Center Study, researchers found four common elements associated with high levels of life satisfaction: good health, a romantic partner, friends, and career.

Today Write about an element from the list above that lends a high level of satisfaction to your life.

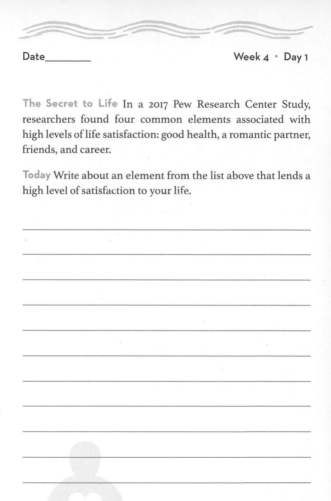

_____

_____

_____

_____

_____

_____

_____

_____

_____

_____

_____

_____

Granting Wishes Dr. Jonathan Tudge's study on how children (ages 7–14) express gratitude reveals that some children offer an item they value, such as their own toys, to the giver who has granted them a wish. However, other children are more thoughtful about what would be important or valuable to give the wish granter, making their reciprocity more meaningful. Other studies indicate that adults may miss this "meaningful" aspect of children's reciprocity.

Today Consider your day: What meaningful gesture, favor, or wish can you bestow on just one person? Write about what makes your choice meaningful to the recipient.

_____

_____

_____

_____

_____

_____

_____

_____

_____

_____

Clock Game A gratitude practice can take different shapes and forms. Journaling is just one of them. Dr. Brené Brown found a very interesting, tangible practice among her study participants: They would select a sequence of numbers, such as 1, 2, 3, 4, which coincide with 12:34 p.m. At that time each day they would say something—out loud—for which they were grateful.

Today Set a time today just to take on this challenge. Write down a specific time, below, and set your watch or calendar as a reminder to state your gratitude out loud. Also, feel free to write your first statement of gratitude here.

_____

_____

_____

_____

_____

_____

_____

_____

_____

Gotta Have It Now Researchers have found that patience fosters self-control. Notoriously impulsive behaviors, such as compulsive shopping, spending more money than you have, overeating, and smoking, can be reduced by using simple gratitude exercises to curb those impulsive behaviors.

Today Write about an aspect of your life where you'd like to exercise more patience and how that might make your life better.

➤ You're not alone. Everyone has something to work on!

_____

_____

_____

_____

_____

_____

_____

_____

_____

_____

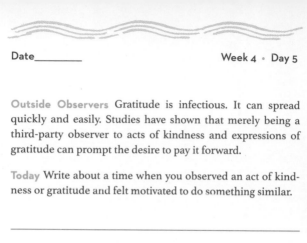

Outside Observers Gratitude is infectious. It can spread quickly and easily. Studies have shown that merely being a third-party observer to acts of kindness and expressions of gratitude can prompt the desire to pay it forward.

Today Write about a time when you observed an act of kindness or gratitude and felt motivated to do something similar.

_____

_____

_____

_____

_____

_____

_____

_____

_____

_____

_____

_____

_____

Threefold Impact People who are aware of the positive effects of gratitude are more likely to partake in the following three behaviors, which also prolong and deepen their enjoyment of relationships:

* *"Find" suitable candidates for future relationships.*
* *"Remind" themselves of the good things in their current relationships.*
* *"Bind" themselves to those partners and friends by making them feel appreciated.*

Today Consider the effect that the Threefold Impact might have had on one of your closest relationships. Write about how the "find," "remind," and "bind" theory has influenced the relationship's dynamic.

_____

_____

_____

_____

_____

_____

_____

_____

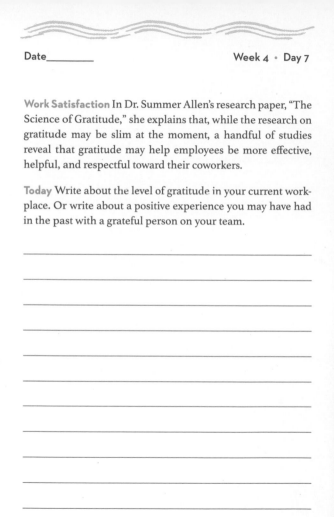

Work Satisfaction In Dr. Summer Allen's research paper, "The Science of Gratitude," she explains that, while the research on gratitude may be slim at the moment, a handful of studies reveal that gratitude may help employees be more effective, helpful, and respectful toward their coworkers.

Today Write about the level of gratitude in your current workplace. Or write about a positive experience you may have had in the past with a grateful person on your team.

_____

_____

_____

_____

_____

_____

_____

_____

_____

_____

_____

_____

_____

Setting Your Intention

> *"These two people are hard to find in the world. Which*
> *two? The one who is first to do a kindness, and the one*
> *who is grateful and thankful for a kindness done."*
>
> —The Buddha, from the *Anguttara Nikaya*

Both the kind and the grateful person are indeed rare.

Today Write about a person you admire for both their kindness and their ability to be grateful. What part of their makeup do you wish to emulate today? Write a simple statement that could look like this: *My intention is to embody the best qualities of Joan, which are* [fill in the blanks].

_____

_____

_____

_____

_____

_____

_____

_____

_____

Origin of Thanksgiving In October 1863, in the middle of the American Civil War, President Abraham Lincoln made Thanksgiving an official holiday as a means of unifying the nation. Take a few moments to consider how grossly commercial this holiday has now become and reflect on Lincoln's expression of gratitude for a multitude of blessings and bounty in the midst of a civil war in the hope of restoring peace, harmony, and tranquility in the nation.

Today Consider the current political environment, the tenor at your workplace, or the milieu in your home or community. Could any of them use a little bit of thanks-giving? Write down three ways that you can express gratitude in any of these situations to help everyone move forward.

_____

_____

_____

_____

_____

_____

_____

_____

Bighearted Love Expressing self-gratitude is as important as expressing gratitude to others. We will start a monthly reminder to show gratitude for the amazing, talented person you are.

Today Write down three things you're most proud of having achieved.

_____

_____

_____

_____

_____

_____

_____

_____

_____

_____

_____

_____

Folding It In One of my friends, a mother, told me that she *folds good dreams* into her children's pajamas. I love the concept of *folding* goodness, gratitude, and happiness into whatever I'm doing. It strikes me as a magical combination of not just expressing gratitude verbally, but taking a symbolic action, even one as simple as folding it into your bedsheets. Neatly fold and tuck in the corners, saying, *I am grateful for my warm, comfortable bed. Thank you.*

Today Write about how you could seamlessly integrate this principle into your day today.

➤ Dare I suggest folding gratitude into your next load of laundry?

_____

_____

_____

_____

_____

_____

_____

_____

Awareness of Benefactors A benefactor is a person or entity that gives you something that you haven't necessarily "earned"—a gift outright. A benefactor could be God, the cosmos, another human, an animal, or nature, for example.

Today Write about who or what you perceive to be a recent benefactor. How do they operate in your life? A random stranger was a pivotal benefactor for me several years ago. Think broadly about this question.

_____

_____

_____

_____

_____

_____

_____

_____

_____

_____

_____

That Special Intervention Psychologists and researchers Robert Emmons and Michael McCullough define *gratitude* as the perception of a positive outcome that is not necessarily deserved or earned, thanks to another person.

Today Write about a positive outcome that seemingly came out of nowhere, and for which you are still grateful.

➤ **The positive outcome may be material or nonmaterial.**

_____

_____

_____

_____

_____

_____

_____

_____

_____

_____

_____

_____

Grief Reflection Grief is a very real emotion and process. Mourning the loss of someone close to you, while recalling, with gratitude, a positive experience or lesson that you learned from them in the past, allows you to turn a somber situation into one of comfort and even joy.

Today Write about a positive experience or lesson you may have learned from someone who meant a lot to you, and for which you are grateful, as you mourned their loss.

_____

_____

_____

_____

_____

_____

_____

_____

_____

_____

GRACE Results The Gratitude Research in Acute Coronary Events (GRACE) study, conducted just a few years ago, determined that individuals with higher levels of gratitude and optimism had biomarkers indicating lower levels of inflammation and improved blood vessel function.

Today Write a note of thanks to your body for taking care of you.

_____

_____

_____

_____

_____

_____

_____

_____

_____

_____

_____

_____

_____

Recent Memory In a conversation between two female colleagues, who were having a very rough go of it at work, one said to the other, "I admire your coolness in that meeting. I mean, there's no way I could have done that." The other woman looked at her shoes and then listed all the things she could have done better. Unfortunately, this is a common pattern; people deflect a compliment and subconsciously try to convince the person who made the complimentary observation that the compliment is undeserved, instead of just saying thank you.

Today Write a short list of attributes that others have complimented you on recently. If there's a pattern, i.e., if people tell you that you're patient, circle that word on your list. Take a deep breath and practice self-gratitude by writing *Thank you*, [insert your own name], at the bottom of the page.

_____

_____

_____

_____

_____

_____

_____

Bold Beans Being able to choose what we want to eat or drink is an enviable position to be in, and it's something we may take for granted. Every morning I place my tiny espresso pot on the stove and breathe in the glorious aroma as it brews. The ritual of making an Americano, while still in my bathrobe, culminates with a soft *thank you* as I take the first sip. It's heavenly.

Today Write about a gratitude ritual you could establish as a part of your daily routine.

_____

_____

_____

_____

_____

_____

_____

_____

_____

_____

_____

Three Functions Positive Psychology researchers define the three main functions of gratitude as:

1. a moral *barometer*, reminds us to see the kind acts of others;

2. a moral *motivator*, encourages the concept of "paying it forward";

3. a moral *reinforcer*, prompts us to repeat acts of kindness.

Today Take a look at yourself: Write about the function of gratitude that you exercise most often. What happens as you express gratitude? Do you "size up" people in terms of the kind acts they perform? Are you eager to pay gratitude forward? Are you motivated to do more?

_____

_____

_____

_____

_____

_____

_____

_____

Thorns and All

> *"Some people are always grumbling because roses*
> *have thorns; I am thankful that thorns have roses."*
>
> —Jean-Baptiste Alphonse Karr, 1808–1890,
> French critic, journalist, and novelist

Today Write about a situation that seemed to be full of impediments, but actually brought something beautiful and amazing into your world.

_____

_____

_____

_____

_____

_____

_____

_____

_____

_____

_____

_____

What If? Mental subtraction, known as the "George Bailey Effect" (inspired by the 1946 movie *It's a Wonderful Life*), is a gratitude technique that asks you to consider what you would have missed (that is, how your life would have been worse) if an actual positive event (like meeting the love of your life or getting the job you've always wanted) had never happened.

Today Write about a recent positive event as if it never occurred. What would you have missed by not having had this experience?

_____

_____

_____

_____

_____

_____

_____

_____

_____

_____

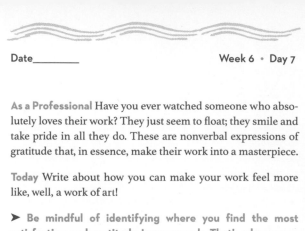

As a Professional Have you ever watched someone who absolutely loves their work? They just seem to float; they smile and take pride in all they do. These are nonverbal expressions of gratitude that, in essence, make their work into a masterpiece.

Today Write about how you can make your work feel more like, well, a work of art!

➤ Be mindful of identifying where you find the most satisfaction and gratitude in your work. That's where your masterpiece will come from.

_____

_____

_____

_____

_____

_____

_____

_____

_____

_____

_____

Introducing GIA Gratitude in Action (GIA) contributes to the gratitude cycle, when you perform deliberate acts of gratitude, on a regular basis, to spread goodness in your life. You can offer gratitude to others beyond a "thank you" or merely writing a gratitude entry in this journal. Expressing gratitude through actions is like sprinkling a little bit of happiness dust wherever you go. We will start this practice next week.

Today Write one to three ways you could show gratitude to another person that doesn't involve a thank-you. Be creative!

Outside Your Control Those who accept life's challenges know that whatever happens to them doesn't matter as much as how they handle those challenges. If the train is late or the bus skips a stop, they stay calm, read a book, and continue on their journey. If someone is rude to them, they remember that other people may have issues affecting their current state of mind. They do not allow circumstances that are outside their control to ruin their day. Circumventing distraction allows them to focus more on the good around them.

Today Can you shrug it off? Write about your level of acceptance of life's challenges.

_____

_____

_____

_____

_____

_____

_____

_____

_____

_____

A Renewed Appreciation If there is a positive side to the Covid-19 pandemic, it is this: The crisis has supplied a reset point for humanity. While we were in quarantine and limiting our engagement with other people, the isolation and quiet opened us up to who and what are truly important to us. We may not have been 100 percent conscious of those new understandings as we were making them, but as we step into the "new normal," it's crucial to acknowledge them: They represent an unfolding of gratitude and the lessons learned from it.

Today Reflect on your quiet time during the Covid-19 pandemic. List three to five things you have decided to limit, or let go of altogether, even after the crisis has passed. List three to five things that you took for granted before the crisis happened, and for which you now feel deep gratitude.

_____

_____

_____

_____

_____

_____

_____

_____

Changing Your Perspective Training yourself to be grateful will change your perspective on people and life. If you feel it is demeaning to be helped by others, then your gratitude for their actions may also feel demeaning. However, if you trust others who give to you, without questioning their motives, then gratitude feels like a wonderful, noble way to navigate the world.

Today Write about how you feel about others helping you. Be honest about where you find yourself in this process.

_____

_____

_____

_____

_____

_____

_____

_____

_____

_____

Three Teachings Carol Zaleski, a professor of world religions, has noted that in East Asian societies, where the "Three Teachings" (Confucian, Daoist, Buddhist) commingle with local spiritual traditions, "Gratitude is the grammar of life." Zaleski goes on to say: "The one thing gratitude must not be, the world's religions tell us, is a legal obligation, an obsequious bargain or a bribe; for gratitude is the response to a gratuitous gift that can be repaid only with another gift, or with the apt gesture or word of thanksgiving."

Today Write about a time when you may not have repaid a generous gesture with a pay-it-forward action or a simple thank-you. Consider how you may be able to do so today.

_____

_____

_____

_____

_____

_____

_____

_____

_____

_____

Shift Your Gears Gratitude has been described as a *gearshift* by author Joan Borysenko. It acts as a mechanism to move our minds "from obsession to peacefulness, from stuckness to creativity, from fear to love." A more relaxed mind is a by-product of living with gratitude.

Today Write about a gearshift moment when feeling gratitude completely changed your perspective and attitude.

_____

_____

_____

_____

_____

_____

_____

_____

_____

_____

_____

_____

_____

Recognizing Beauty

"The more grateful I am, the more beauty I see."

—Mary Davis, 1954– , Irish activist

Today Write about something you never saw as beautiful, until recently, when your perspective changed in some way.

_____

_____

_____

_____

_____

_____

_____

_____

_____

_____

_____

_____

_____

_____

Gratitude in Action #1 Offer a smile to a friend or a stranger as an acknowledgment of their very existence in your life. Receiving a smile releases the happiness hormone dopamine. Mother Teresa of Calcutta once said, "Every time you smile at someone, it is an action of love, a gift to that person, a beautiful thing."

Today Make a list of people with whom you'd like to share your happiness, gratitude, and love through a smile.

_____

_____

_____

_____

_____

_____

_____

_____

_____

_____

_____

Savor the Moment Researchers have found that savoring the moments of life is a critical element in well-being. In other words, constantly being aware of how fortunate we are is the key to happiness!

Today Write about one of the most important moments of your life—something that you still savor and which makes you smile and feel happy that *it* happened, whenever you think about it.

_____

_____

_____

_____

_____

_____

_____

_____

_____

_____

_____

Relationship Measures Many researchers have touted the connection between gratitude and a positive partnership, including romantic partnerships. Expressions of gratitude toward your partner motivate them to extend the same kindness to you and to recognize your best qualities.

Today Write about your experience with gratitude in your partnership. Which of your partner's best qualities have you acknowledged with gratitude recently? Which of your partner's best qualities can you acknowledge today?

➤ Partnerships can also be forged in your place of business.

_____

_____

_____

_____

_____

_____

_____

_____

Working with an Evaluation Scale #1 Researchers who developed the Expressions of Gratitude in Relationships measure use a simple three-statement evaluation to determine the level of gratitude between partners. How would you assess yourself using a 5-point scale, from 1 ("never") to 5 ("very frequently")?

Here's the first statement:

I express my appreciation for the things my partner does for me.

Today Write down your assessment measure on the scale of 1 to 5 in response to this statement. Then write about something your partner does for you that makes you feel grateful.

_____

_____

_____

_____

_____

_____

_____

_____

_____

Working with an Evaluation Scale #2 Here is the second statement from the Expressions of Gratitude in Relationships measure:

I let my partner know that I value him/her.

Today Using the same 5-point scale as on the previous day, write down your assessment and how you let your partner know that you value them. Give yourself bonus points if you can identify the warm, positive character trait that you see in them at this moment.

_____

_____

_____

_____

_____

_____

_____

_____

_____

_____

Working with an Evaluation Scale #3 This is the last statement from the Expressions of Gratitude in Relationships measure:

Today Write down your assessment and describe how you acknowledged your partner recently.

_____

_____

_____

_____

_____

_____

_____

_____

_____

_____

_____

_____

_____

Unicorn Days It's easy to be grateful when things are going well, you're gliding through life, and everything seems wonderful. Those are "unicorn days." But what about the days that are stressful, frustrating, and not so full of magic? In those moments, pause and say out loud, "I am grateful for . . ." This deliberate action interrupts a negative pattern of thought, shifting your focus to something more positive.

Today Recall a stressful part of a recent day. Write down three "I am grateful for . . ." statements now.

➤ I use this technique a lot when I'm trying to drive in New York City. It's never easy, but this method helps keep me calm and reminds me that not everyone is a bad driver.

_____

_____

_____

_____

_____

_____

_____

_____

_____

The Intention of Waking In the Jewish tradition, giving thanks for the mere feat of waking up each morning is cause for gratitude, considering what the alternative could be!

Today Write your intention for the next few weeks and how you will animate it. For example, make it a practice for the next week to set your intention to be grateful as soon as you open your eyes and stretch out your arms to meet each and every new day.

➤ Setting an intention in this way puts you in the gratitude cycle for the entire day.

_____

_____

_____

_____

_____

_____

_____

_____

_____

Benefits to the Grateful Person Cornell University social psychologist Thomas Gilovich has found that grateful people, in contrast to those who are not grateful, experience a greater sense of well-being, improved sleep, fewer doctor visits, and an increased sense of meaning in their lives.

Today Write about how your current gratitude practice is impacting your life for the better.

_____

_____

_____

_____

_____

_____

_____

_____

_____

_____

_____

_____

Recent Memory Marking milestones, big or small, is part of a gratitude practice. Review your day, or the previous day. What did you do well?

Today Write a list of three to five things you did well in the past few days.

_____

_____

_____

_____

_____

_____

_____

_____

_____

_____

_____

_____

_____

Satisfaction and Happiness Sixteen percent of Americans surveyed by the Pew Research Center mentioned good health for themselves and those around them, when describing what gives them a sense of meaning and satisfaction. Some were grateful for their own good health, despite their age, or thankful for wonderful helpers, such as doctors, who care for them or a family member. Overall, those who ranked their own health or having a healthy family as a high priority placed themselves 11 percent higher on the life satisfaction scale than other Americans.

Today Write about how good health is meaningful to you and what it allows you to do.

_____

_____

_____

_____

_____

_____

_____

_____

_____

_____

Forgiveness Matters Well-being has been positively correlated with forgiveness and gratitude. A study of 72 participants, by Loren Toussaint and Philip Friedman, found that forgiveness coupled with gratitude, either for giving or receiving forgiveness, promoted well-being in the study participants.

Today Express your gratitude in writing for a gesture of forgiveness given to you in the past or one that you've given yourself.

_____

_____

_____

_____

_____

_____

_____

_____

_____

_____

_____

_____

Upward Spiral Psychologists Robert A. Emmons and Michael McCullough conducted a study on the effects of a grateful outlook on physical and psychological well-being. Their conclusion was that participants who focused on all the good in their lives improved their sense of well-being more than those who focused on hassles and social comparisons.

Today Write about the *goodness* that allows you to see, do, and have certain special experiences.

➤ It could be traveling, the ability to bake fresh bread, or simply sitting in a garden and breathing in the fragrance of flowers.

_____

_____

_____

_____

_____

_____

_____

_____

_____

_____

Pairing Them Up Psychologists Leah Dickens and David DeSteno's research on gratitude links the ability to exhibit self-control with an increase in patience. Grateful people are more comfortable delaying gratification, when necessary, than those with lower levels of gratitude.

Today Write about your comfort level in delaying gratification. Consider a current indulgence you'd like to partake in. Can you patiently wait for that new iPhone, your next date, or that chocolate brownie?

_____

_____

_____

_____

_____

_____

_____

_____

_____

_____

_____

_____

Gratitude in Action #2 When I was at the market today, I saw a sign advertising a "two for one" deal for hummus. Since I don't need two containers just for myself and my husband, I turned to the woman who was standing behind me at the checkout and explained my situation. She laughed when I offered her the free container. "Sure, that would be lovely," she said. "I'll take that off your hands."

Today Write about a time when someone had more than enough of something for their own use and was willing to share it with you. How did that make you feel? How can you extend that type of generosity today?

_____

_____

_____

_____

_____

_____

_____

_____

_____

_____

Nonverbal Gestures President John F. Kennedy memorably said, "As we express our gratitude, we must never forget that the highest appreciation is not to utter words, but to live by them." We must embody gratitude in all aspects of our being.

Today Write about how you radiate gratitude in just being who you are and how you interact with others.

_____

_____

_____

_____

_____

_____

_____

_____

_____

_____

_____

_____

_____

Rewiring the Circuits Researchers at Indiana University–Bloomington have defined gratitude as not just an experience, but also an expression.

Today Write about ways you can express gratitude, other than by saying "thank you."

➤ These ideas will be as unique as you are. Have fun with this exercise!

_____

_____

_____

_____

_____

_____

_____

_____

_____

_____

_____

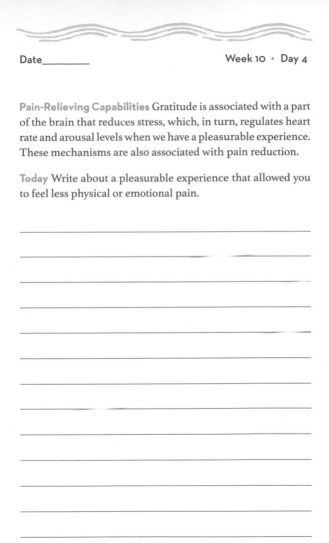

Pain-Relieving Capabilities Gratitude is associated with a part of the brain that reduces stress, which, in turn, regulates heart rate and arousal levels when we have a pleasurable experience. These mechanisms are also associated with pain reduction.

Today Write about a pleasurable experience that allowed you to feel less physical or emotional pain.

_____

_____

_____

_____

_____

_____

_____

_____

_____

_____

_____

_____

Ripples of Gratitude Researchers have found that grateful people not only extend their appreciation to others who may have enriched a moment in their lives, they also pay it forward—sometimes to a total stranger or even someone who may not have had anything to do with the original act of kindness.

Today Write about someone who has been a benefactor in your life. How did their helpfulness change your day or an important aspect of your life?

_____

_____

_____

_____

_____

_____

_____

_____

_____

_____

_____

Strangers among Us When living in a state of gratitude, individuals will help total strangers without a second thought.

Today Write about the last time you acknowledged a complete stranger by opening a door for them, greeting them warmly, or paying for their coffee?

_____

_____

_____

_____

_____

_____

_____

_____

_____

_____

_____

_____

_____

_____

Making a Social Impact Empirical research has concluded
that social emotions, such as gratitude, play a part in reshaping societal behaviors. Gratitude fosters relationships and
a mind-set that forgives short-term setbacks in our relationships, based on the underlying belief that a long-term relationship will yield more good for both parties: Forgiving a
mistake today can build a stronger relationship down the road.

Today Write about the last time you observed several people
demonstrating gratitude to one another at work or in another
group setting.

_____

_____

_____

_____

_____

_____

_____

_____

_____

_____

_____

Gratitude in Action #3 Who doesn't love freshly baked, warm cookies? Make a batch for a teacher, a nurse, a volunteer fire-fighter, or anyone who might simply love the gesture, as a thank-you for all they do.

Today If you're not a baker, you can buy a small treat to give away. Write about the recipient and why you chose to give them a treat.

➤ **Sarah Kieffer's recipe for Pan-Banging Good Chocolate Chip Cookies can be found online. They're amazing!**

_____

_____

_____

_____

_____

_____

_____

_____

_____

_____

_____

Commercial Slant When a business focuses on resolving and relieving their customers' pain points, they are showing a nonverbal form of gratitude. The subtext is "I think I can help you with X, Y, or Z. Thank you for trusting me."

Today Write about a nonverbal form of gratitude that you can weave into your work for whoever the end user may be. Remember: Everyone has one.

_____

_____

_____

_____

_____

_____

_____

_____

_____

_____

_____

_____

A Friend's Safe Harbor Listening to a friend, or just showing up for them in a time of need, is a nonverbal form of communication that expresses how much you value their friendship, as well as showing love and the willingness to truly hear them.

Today Write about how you can improve your listening skills or be more attentive to the needs of others.

_____

_____

_____

_____

_____

_____

_____

_____

_____

_____

_____

Shifting Focus Zoketsu Norman Fischer, a Zen Buddhist priest, teacher, and writer, points out how we often overlook what is working in our lives, unless we take a moment to acknowledge what we *do* have that is good and satisfying. He has said, "We take our life, we take existence, for granted. We take it as a given, and then we complain that it isn't working out as we wanted it to. But why should we be here in the first place? Why should we exist at all?"

Today Take a moment to consider all the things that may not be working in your life right now. It's OK. Take a deep breath, quiet your mind, and write a gratitude statement for three positive things you've learned about yourself in the midst of recent chaos.

_____

_____

_____

_____

_____

_____

_____

_____

_____

Default Mechanism Sometimes we minimize our expressions of gratitude by focusing on what we do not have. Jennifer Urezzio, founder and spiritual director of Soul Language, calls this a "drive-by gratitude." She explains, "A drive-by gratitude is like, 'God, thank you for blah-blah-blah, but by the way, I don't have blah-blah-blah.' "

Today Write about a recent drive-by gratitude you may have offered. Backtrack and rewrite the initial gratitude statement, along with two more that deal with what you *have* rather than a complaint about what you don't have.

➤ *A good one might be Oops! I'm grateful to be aware that I may have a few drive-by gratitude episodes in my past. I had no idea!*

_____

_____

_____

_____

_____

_____

_____

_____

_____

Polished Rocks Several years ago, I was given three polished stones. Each stone has one of three words—*love, patience,* or *gratitude*—inscribed on it. I instantly loved them! I was instructed to put the stones someplace where I'd see them every day as a reminder to practice the principles that are engraved on them. The stones were placed on my bathroom sink. For more than ten years, as I've brushed my teeth every morning, their simple messages have made me smile.

Today Write down three words that you could put on three small rocks or stones. Where would you place them so that you could see them every day? Or, if you would like to give away a stone with a simple one-word message, who would you give it to?

_____

_____

_____

_____

_____

_____

_____

_____

Experiencing Delight Starting on his 42nd birthday, the poet Ross Gay wrote one essay a day, for one year, detailing the things, people, places, and activities that delighted him on a daily basis. The result was *The Book of Delight: Essays*, an experiment in paying attention to the things that brought him joy, and which he then shared with his readers. In essence, writing the book was his gratitude practice.

Today How does the word *delight* feel to you? Make a list of three things that delighted your senses yesterday or today.

_____

_____

_____

_____

_____

_____

_____

_____

_____

_____

Gratitude in Action #4 Acknowledge the work of a colleague with a Post-it® note that says, "Thank you for all you do," along with a piece of their favorite chocolate.

Today Write about another way that you could show your gratitude to a colleague.

_____

_____

_____

_____

_____

_____

_____

_____

_____

_____

_____

_____

_____

_____

Increased Honesty Experiments conducted by psychologist David DeSteno and his colleagues at Northeastern University found that employees who are grateful are dishonest 27 percent of the time, while those who could not recount a time when they felt happy about an event in their lives were dishonest 56 percent of the time, almost twice as often. Dr. DeSteno summed up the results of the experiments, however, by saying, "Gratitude worked the same for everyone: a few moments spent feeling grateful dramatically improved the moral choices people made."

Today Write about how gratitude helps you maintain your moral compass.

_____

_____

_____

_____

_____

_____

_____

_____

_____

_____

Avoiding the Wrecking Ball Anger and frustration can overtake you in a situation where you may feel unappreciated. During these times, you have the potential to become a wrecking ball and knock down everything you've worked for. So it's important to remember to quiet your mind and breathe deeply a few times to release the internal pressure. Then ask yourself: What gift has this situation brought to my life? What have I learned from it?

Today Write about a positive gift or lesson you may have gained. For example, did a major challenge at work help you to appreciate your talents or feel more confident about supporting a position that you may not have had the courage to defend in the past? As uncomfortable for you as that may have been, are you proud of your inner strength?

_____

_____

_____

_____

_____

_____

_____

Fill in the Blank Write an email, send a text, or tell someone today: "Thank you so much for doing X. It means the world to me."

Today Write three of these statements below.

_____

_____

_____

_____

_____

_____

_____

_____

_____

_____

_____

_____

_____

Frequent Patterns The deeper you dive into your gratitude practice, the more likely it is that you will begin to notice many aspects of the gratitude cycle around you—some more than others. You may see that people are being nicer to one another, more generous, or you may hear a specific gratitude phrase spoken more frequently than before. It's not your imagination, you're observing these things because you now have a heightened awareness of gratitude. This phenomenon is known as the "frequency (or recency) illusion."

Today Write about gratitude frequency patterns you may have picked up on recently.

Colors The color yellow is found everywhere. Yellow tea roses and freesia adorn my dining room table. The gold leaf on the mirror across the room looks so regal. The beautiful sun, as winter moves into the early days of spring, is a lovely pale yellow. Yellow is also the color of amber, like the enchanting eyes of my little gray cat. The list is endless.

Today Write about a color that appeals to you. Make a list of all the things about that color that make you feel appreciation, delight, and gratitude for it.

_____

_____

_____

_____

_____

_____

_____

_____

_____

_____

Childhood Snapshot Positive psychology researchers correlate gratitude with happiness. Gratitude inspires people to experience positive emotions, which helps them enjoy life experiences. This, in turn, boosts their health and ability to recover from adversity, and build stronger relationships. All of which promotes happiness. One way to express gratitude is to be gracious about the past.

Today Write about a positive childhood memory that is still a source of inspiration to you.

_____

_____

_____

_____

_____

_____

_____

_____

_____

_____

The Intention of Enough Some of us may recall the insecurities of adolescence and dwelling on what we didn't have. Those emotions reflect envy and materialism, making them antithetical to gratitude. Set the intention to believe that you are enough and you have enough.

Today Write down your intention statement. Consider this: *I set my intention to focus on the fact that I am enough, no matter what others may think, and that I have plenty of everything in my life. For all of these things I am grateful.*

_____

_____

_____

_____

_____

_____

_____

_____

_____

_____

Long-Lasting Results Genuine expressions of happiness create threads that weave through a lifetime. Researchers studying yearbook photos from 1958 to 1960 found that the people in the photographs whose smiles were authentic had more satisfying marriages and felt a greater sense of well-being 30 years later.

Forced or sarcastic smiles and solemn facial expressions might have been factored into which smiles were viewed as authentic and which seemed disingenuous.

Today Do your own research. Reflect on the general disposition of a person you know who may not be happy, as opposed to one who is happy. Write about that person's ability to find good things in life to be happy about.

_____

_____

_____

_____

_____

_____

_____

_____

The Humble Mind

> *"Pride slays thanksgiving, but a humble mind*
> *is the soil out of which thanks naturally grows.*
> *A proud man is seldom a grateful man for he*
> *never thinks he gets as much as he deserves."*

—Henry Ward Beecher, 1813–1887, American Congregationalist
minister, speaker, social reformer, and abolitionist

Today Write a humble statement of gratitude for a bountiful experience.

_____

_____

_____

_____

_____

_____

_____

_____

_____

_____

Writing Letters University of Indiana researchers conducted an experiment focused on gratitude and its impact on mental health, using three groups of people. They asked the first group to write a gratitude letter once a week; the second group was asked to write about their negative thoughts and feelings; and the third group was instructed to write nothing at all. Hands down, those who practiced gratitude reported signs of better mental health over a 12-week period.

Today You are now roughly 12 weeks into journaling about gratitude. Write about how this practice is transforming your mental health. What positive effects are you experiencing in your overall mood and outlook on life?

_____

_____

_____

_____

_____

_____

_____

_____

_____

Four Thieves Rebecca C. Solom's master's thesis, which she wrote as a student at Eastern Washington University, is titled "Thieves of Gratitude: Inhibitors of Gratitude." Solom identifies the four biggest inhibitors of gratitude as cynicism; materialism/envy; indebtedness; and narcissism.

Today Write about an inhibitor of gratitude that you may have overcome. How did it previously impact your life?

_____

_____

_____

_____

_____

_____

_____

_____

_____

_____

_____

_____

_____

_____

Celebrating the Now One of the most transformative aspects of gratitude is that it places us squarely in the moment. That sense of presence helps us acknowledge the value of whatever may be happening in the moment and prolongs being in a positive state. Researcher and psychologist Dr. Robert Emmons points out that dwelling in and appreciating the value of the moment makes it less likely that you'll take it for granted.

Today Reflect on something that you may have taken for granted recently. It could be something very simple. Write about the value it has in your life.

➤ If you're searching for an idea, try writing about your toothbrush or the sweater that keeps you warm.

_____

_____

_____

_____

_____

_____

_____

_____

_____

Love Your Stuff Researchers have found that people who have a high level of gratitude also appreciate the material goods they have. This appreciation helps them to circumvent the endless treadmill of negative materialism—the constant longing for what they don't have.

Today Write a gratitude statement for a material thing that improves your disposition every day.

_____

_____

_____

_____

_____

_____

_____

_____

_____

_____

_____

_____

Gratitude in Action #5 Help a neighbor carry grocery bags from their car or packages from the curb to their doorstep.

Today Write about the person to whom you'd like to extend this kind of gratitude.

➤ If this one isn't feasible for you to do, then carry out a GIA of your own choosing and write about it.

_____

_____

_____

_____

_____

_____

_____

_____

_____

_____

_____

_____

_____

A Stabilizing Factor In his 1759 book *The Theory of Moral Sentiments,* Scottish economist and philosopher Adam Smith wrote that the benevolence of gratitude promotes a general attitude of goodwill among us that helps stabilize society. Is it any wonder that groups of people who have a positive attitude and are grateful are more fun to hang out with?

Today Write about how this phenomenon plays out in the groups of people you spend most of your time with. What, in particular, makes you grateful to be part of such a group?

_____

_____

_____

_____

_____

_____

_____

_____

_____

_____

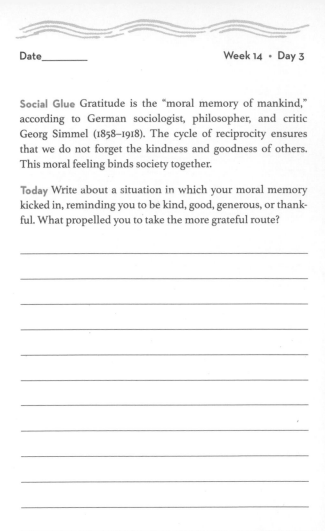

Social Glue Gratitude is the "moral memory of mankind," according to German sociologist, philosopher, and critic Georg Simmel (1858–1918). The cycle of reciprocity ensures that we do not forget the kindness and goodness of others. This moral feeling binds society together.

Today Write about a situation in which your moral memory kicked in, reminding you to be kind, good, generous, or thankful. What propelled you to take the more grateful route?

_____

_____

_____

_____

_____

_____

_____

_____

_____

_____

_____

Date_____

Week 14 · Day 4

Side Effects of Gratitude Studies undertaken by researchers at the University of California–Berkeley revealed that those that who maintain a practice of "count your blessings" or keep a gratitude journal for at least 10 weeks spend more time exercising and have fewer physical complaints than those who focus on daily grievances.

Today Write about any changes in your daily routine that have positively impacted your physical state over the past 14 weeks.

_____

_____

_____

_____

_____

_____

_____

_____

_____

_____

_____

Burnout Remedy A study of a small group of schoolteachers in Hong Kong, by Professor David W. Chan, showed that the tendency to notice and appreciate the big and the small things in life may help protect people from burnout.

Today Write about a lesson you may have learned during a period of burnout or near-burnout. Remember: Having gratitude for even the most difficult times is important.

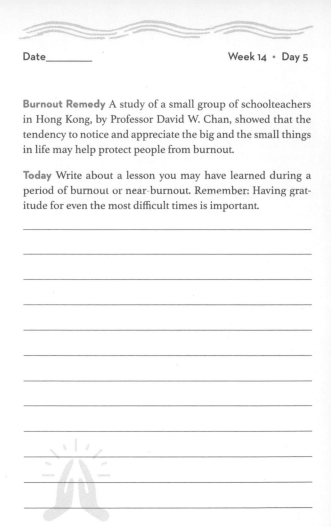

The Seeking Brain We tend to notice things if we've deliberately searched for them. There is an infinite number of
things to be grateful for, such as the freedom in life, the air
we breathe, the way grass feels under bare feet, the color blue,
or the ability to travel freely. Oftentimes, we do not give these
things the attention they deserve unless we consciously think
about them.

Today Using your curiosity and maybe even a little spirit of
adventure, find three things that are new and/or stimulating,
and that have evoked a sense of gratitude in you in the past 24
hours. Write them below.

_____

_____

_____

_____

_____

_____

_____

_____

_____

_____

Unlocking Life's Fullness

> *"Gratitude unlocks the fullness of life. It turns what we have into enough, and more. It turns denial into acceptance, chaos into order, confusion into clarity. It can turn a meal into a feast, a house into a home, a stranger into a friend."*

—Melody Beattie, author of *Codependent No More, Journey to the Heart, The Language of Letting Go,* and many others

Today Reflect on the many aspects of this insight. Write a gratitude statement in response to a portion of Beattie's quote that feels particularly pertinent to your experience.

_____

_____

_____

_____

_____

_____

_____

_____

_____

_____

Gratitude in Action #6 The next time you receive excellent service in a restaurant, make a point of telling the manager that the waitstaff did a fabulous job.

Today Think about an opportunity you may have had recently that would qualify for this GIA. What did you appreciate about the service you received?

_____

_____

_____

_____

_____

_____

_____

_____

_____

_____

_____

_____

Nonverbal Communications The Nguni people have lived in southern Africa for more than 2,000 years. Nonverbal communication of gratitude is an important aspect of their culture. In her book *Nonverbal Communication,* Melanie K. Finney, DePauw University professor of communication, suggests that the Nguni hold their hands in a cupping position to receive a gift because the gesture signals that "The gift you give me means so much that I must hold it in two hands."

Today Write about the most interesting nonverbal expression of gratitude you've experienced.

_____

_____

_____

_____

_____

_____

_____

_____

_____

_____

Parent-Child Connection Andrea Hussong, director of the Center for Developmental Science and a professor of psychology at the University of North Carolina at Chapel Hill, and her colleagues, observed that parents who have high levels of gratitude are more likely to make gratitude part of their child's socialization. Encouraging their children to participate in volunteering and being helpful to others is part of that process.

Today Write about the way your parents encouraged, or did not encourage, you to express gratitude.

_____

_____

_____

_____

_____

_____

_____

_____

_____

_____

_____

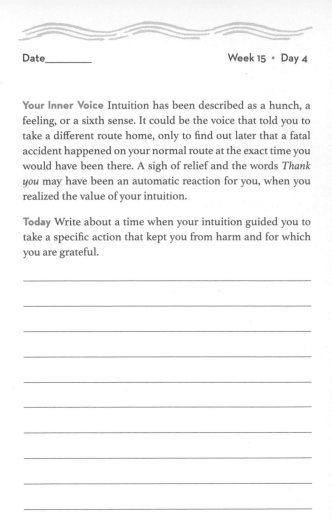

Your Inner Voice Intuition has been described as a hunch, a feeling, or a sixth sense. It could be the voice that told you to take a different route home, only to find out later that a fatal accident happened on your normal route at the exact time you would have been there. A sigh of relief and the words *Thank you* may have been an automatic reaction for you, when you realized the value of your intuition.

Today Write about a time when your intuition guided you to take a specific action that kept you from harm and for which you are grateful.

_____

_____

_____

_____

_____

_____

_____

_____

_____

_____

Pathway to Connectivity Best-selling author, teacher, and modern-day mystic Caroline Myss offers this fluid explanation of the cycle of giving: "The warm glow we get from helping others is not just a good physical feeling—it is the energy of a healing grace that moves between the giver and receiver and blesses both. We need each other. We're not meant to be completely independent, but to give and receive." She adds, "You cannot strive for a healthier more spiritual life if you keep yourself separate and apart from life around you. The journey to *self* also involves the journey of the *other*."

Today Write about your reaction to Myss's ideas about connection and the mutually beneficial aspect of giving to others.

_____

_____

_____

_____

_____

_____

_____

_____

_____

_____

Childlike Eyes Curiosity is a form of wonder, discovery, and acknowledgment of something new that is given to you in the form of an insight, an inspiration, assistance, a gift, or simple happenstance. Approaching your day with the expectation of wonder and curiosity will open your eyes to new experiences.

Today Write about the last time you allowed yourself to view the world around you through childlike eyes, as if everything were new and exciting. Make a point of doing this throughout your day.

_____

_____

_____

_____

_____

_____

_____

_____

_____

_____

_____

Anti-FOMO (Fear of Missing Out) According to Wattpad, the world's largest social network of readers and writers, early Gen Z's (those born between 1995–2015) may be the most stressed-out current demographic. Still, these young people manage to find peace by embracing JOMO (the Joy of Missing Out) by creating a balance between life offline and online, limiting their online time to things that offer more positive takeaways.

Today Write about three sites you visit online that bring you a sense of peace and gratitude.

_____

_____

_____

_____

_____

_____

_____

_____

_____

_____

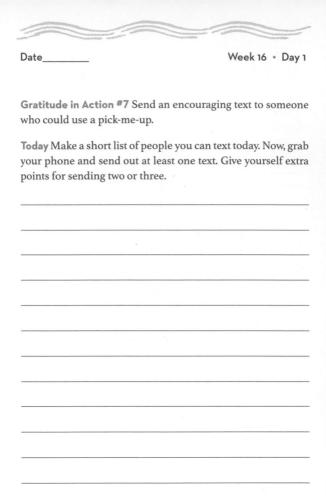

Gratitude in Action #7 Send an encouraging text to someone who could use a pick-me-up.

Today Make a short list of people you can text today. Now, grab your phone and send out at least one text. Give yourself extra points for sending two or three.

_____

_____

_____

_____

_____

_____

_____

_____

_____

_____

_____

_____

_____

Random Acts of Bravery A friend told me that it took every ounce of her being to walk away from a bad relationship. But she did it anyway. It took more than a year for her to heal and muster the courage to say yes to the possibility of finding a healthy, loving relationship again. But she did that, too, regardless of her apprehensions. Summoning the ability to be brave is an event worth celebrating. It is also a way to practice self-gratitude.

Today Write about your last act of bravery.

_____

_____

_____

_____

_____

_____

_____

_____

_____

_____

_____

Creating Partnerships The pivotal emotions of gratitude and love play a significant part in building trust in a relationship. In expressing these emotions you encourage your partner to embody them as well.

Today Write about the roles that gratitude and love play in your current relationships, including those with friends, colleagues, and acquaintances.

_____

_____

_____

_____

_____

_____

_____

_____

_____

_____

_____

_____

_____

Crummy Cortisol Researchers have found that people who express gratitude freely have lower levels of cortisol, the stress hormone, and are more resilient in the face of life's challenges. They tend to bounce back from setbacks more quickly than others.

Today Write a gratitude entry about the last situation that might have caused you stress and anxiety, but did not.

_____

_____

_____

_____

_____

_____

_____

_____

_____

_____

_____

Keep It In Context "The key is to view the unfortunate things that happen to us *in the context of gratitude*," says attorney and writer Meerabelle Dey. "For example, if I am grateful for all the good things in my life—a place to live, my health, financial security—then a missed train is not a big deal."

Today Using Meerabelle's "key," write your own statement about a recent disappointment, and your response to it.

_____

_____

_____

_____

_____

_____

_____

_____

_____

_____

_____

_____

_____

Shifting Your Gratitude Psychologist Thomas Gilovich's research has found that some experiential opportunities promote more gratitude and make people happier and even more altruistic than others that actually "cost" more. For example, while we can't always afford to go on vacation where or when we want to, there are plenty of accessible places, such as parks, bike paths, hiking trails, and clean beaches to enjoy—for free. There's also no charge for creating a special experience with a child or a friend by spending active quality time together.

Today Write about a low- to no-cost experience you can create with people you love.

_____

_____

_____

_____

_____

_____

_____

_____

_____

_____

I Am Grateful Spin During cancer treatment, a patient twirled the ring on his left hand, quietly saying, "*Despite all of this, I am grateful for my life.*" As chemotherapy dragged on, month after month, the patient added more to the list of things that made him feel grateful. According to Jenny R. Craig, LCSW, inventor and creator of the Grateful Ring™, the process of spinning something like a ring, while holding a grateful thought for 20 seconds, triggers the release of chemicals in the brain that help us feel better by cementing feelings of gratitude.

Today Write about an item, a scent, or a visual cue that helps you remember to be grateful.

➤ **If you don't have a ring to spin on your finger, you can use another tangible cue, such as a polished stone or a seashell, that you hold in your hand.**

_____

_____

_____

_____

_____

_____

_____

_____

The Intention of Influence It has been said that a person who has learned how to be grateful "pays forward" kindness and knows that their influence will spread positivity and gratitude to others in everything they do.

Today Write a possible intention for today. As an example: *My intention is to spread kindness and respect to every person I meet, even if it's just a smile.* Or you can customize an intention statement of your own.

_____

_____

_____

_____

_____

_____

_____

_____

_____

_____

_____

Prosocial Currency Economist Robert Frank coined the term the *commitment problem* to describe the reluctance of an individual to invest their time and energy in a relationship, out of fear that they may never receive anything in return. It is also a term researchers apply to people who are fearful of investing their gratitude in others.

Today Write about an experience that you may have had with this fear. Who was involved and why were you concerned that there might not be an equal investment of gratitude?

_____

_____

_____

_____

_____

_____

_____

_____

_____

_____

_____

Reciprocity Expectation Gratitude researchers have found that when someone is thanked for their help, the person receiving the help is more inclined to offer a favor in return, even if that favor, in the short term, may come at some expense (literally or figuratively). Ultimately, the exchange helps build trust in a relationship.

Today Write about an experience, such as the one described above, where you helped or did a favor for a person who has helped you in the past. How did that experience positively impact your relationship?

_____

_____

_____

_____

_____

_____

_____

_____

_____

_____

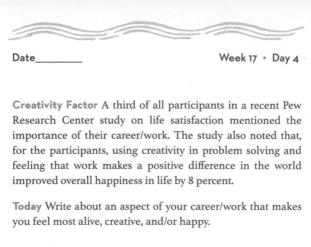

Creativity Factor A third of all participants in a recent Pew Research Center study on life satisfaction mentioned the importance of their career/work. The study also noted that, for the participants, using creativity in problem solving and feeling that work makes a positive difference in the world improved overall happiness in life by 8 percent.

Today Write about an aspect of your career/work that makes you feel most alive, creative, and/or happy.

_____

_____

_____

_____

_____

_____

_____

_____

_____

_____

_____

A Toast on Sandy Shores Standing on the white sand of a nearby beach, four friends raise their glasses to the skies: "We are so profoundly grateful that we are all happy, healthy, and have navigated the Covid-19 crisis with a smile on our faces, a surplus of toilet paper, and laughter in our hearts." The friends laugh out loud and, as their wineglasses clink, affirm their mutual gratitude: "We are so fortunate to have had each other to keep our sanity over these past months!"

Today Write about the people or a person you were most grateful to have been supported by during the pandemic and why. Feel free to toast them in your journal entry or, if it's safe, in person.

_____

_____

_____

_____

_____

_____

_____

_____

_____

_____

Making School Cool Most of us have had teachers who made a big impact on our lives. I am forever grateful to the ones who taught me that it is cool to be creative and smart; amazing to be a girl; and that just being myself is the most precious calling card I can offer.

Today Write a gratitude entry for a special teacher in your life. Which of their lessons have you carried with you into adulthood? Why are those lessons so profound and personal?

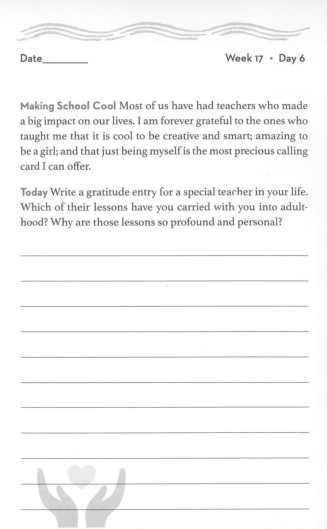

Self-Marketing Gratitude has an undeniable ripple effect, connecting like-minded people, which makes it a great networking tool online. @TheSocialNurse, Carol Bush, impact & innovation director of Susan G. Komen® Race for the Cure in Kansas & Western Missouri, has tweeted, "Showing gratitude is the most effective social media practice."

Today Write a tweet or social media post that focuses on gratitude.

➤ There are many famous quotes and nuggets in this journal as well as the *Resiliency Journal* which serve as prompts for this exercise.

➤ Please tag us #GratitudeJournal @MariaGamb to build your momentum in this medium.

_____

_____

_____

_____

_____

_____

_____

_____

_____

Gratitude in Action #8 Yield the remote to your significant other. Allow them to watch the show of their choice tonight. Sharing is also an attribute of giving.

Today Write about other things you can share with your partner and why those things may be important to them.

➤ I promise, you'll be able to hand over that remote and share many other things with your partner, too. Just remember how much you love and appreciate them.

_____

_____

_____

_____

_____

_____

_____

_____

_____

_____

_____

_____

Child's Play Culture and environment have been proven to influence the development of children. Researchers at the University of North Carolina at Greensboro found that children who are educated in an environment that communicates honor, respect, and gratitude, and a culture of character, had a 21 percent higher ability than other children to express gratitude, as well as a 35 percent higher ability to behave honorably and make correct moral choices on their own.

Today Write a gratitude entry that relates to how your environment or culture has influenced you to "do the right thing" without being prompted.

_____

_____

_____

_____

_____

_____

_____

_____

_____

_____

Workplace Culture How do you influence the culture at your workplace? Take a page from the children at Greensboro (North Carolina) Montessori School and use their simple formula for promoting a culture of gratitude: Treat others with respect and make moral decisions that are motivated by a genuine desire to do the right thing.

Today Write about how you can help create an attitude of gratitude in your workplace.

➤ **Developing a positive and appreciative environment starts with you. Be the example that others follow.**

_____

_____

_____

_____

_____

_____

_____

_____

_____

_____

_____

Motivating Each Other According to Adam Grant, PhD, professor of psychology at the Wharton School of the University of Pennsylvania, and Francesca Gino, professor of business administration at Harvard Business School, people are more likely to help someone they've helped before, if the recipient of their help has thanked them. Mutual gratitude evokes feelings of social worth for both parties—the feeling that others reciprocate kindness.

Today Take a moment today to consider and then write about how you felt the last time you were thanked for something you did for another person.

_____

_____

_____

_____

_____

_____

_____

_____

_____

Three Findings According to Monica Y. Bartlett, associate professor and chair of the psychology department at Gonzaga University, and David DeSteno, professor of psychology at Northeastern University, the positive social impact of gratitude is threefold:

* *Gratitude promotes the desire to help others.*

* *Grateful people acknowledge and help those who have helped them.*

* *Grateful people often help others without the need for reciprocity.*

Today Pick one of the three statements about the social impact of gratitude above, and write about how it has become part of your daily practice.

_____

_____

_____

_____

_____

_____

_____

_____

Benefits to Others Dr. Thomas Gilovich, professor of psychology at Cornell University, found that the greatest benefit to those who are around a grateful person is engaging with that person's "best self."

Today Write about what your best self looks like.

_____

_____

_____

_____

_____

_____

_____

_____

_____

_____

_____

_____

_____

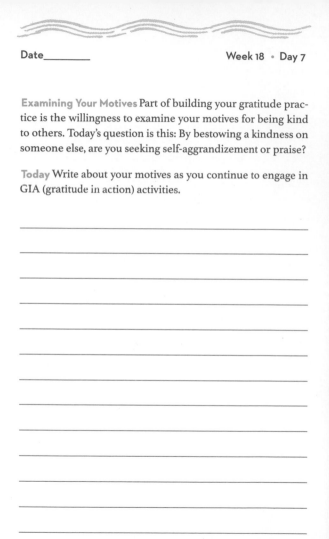

Examining Your Motives Part of building your gratitude practice is the willingness to examine your motives for being kind to others. Today's question is this: By bestowing a kindness on someone else, are you seeking self-aggrandizement or praise?

Today Write about your motives as you continue to engage in GIA (gratitude in action) activities.

_____

_____

_____

_____

_____

_____

_____

_____

_____

_____

_____

_____

_____

_____

Gratitude in Action #9 Hold a door open for two different people this week.

Today Write about how it felt the last time someone held a door open for you.

_____

_____

_____

_____

_____

_____

_____

_____

_____

_____

_____

_____

_____

_____

_____

More Creates More If you're the recipient of gratitude on a regular basis—in contrast to those who don't experience as much gratitude—that fosters even more prosocial behaviors, such as helping friends as well as strangers.

Today Write about how receiving regular expressions of gratitude from others has affected your willingness to help others.

_____

_____

_____

_____

_____

_____

_____

_____

_____

_____

_____

_____

_____

The Call to Strangers During 9/11, New York City was flooded with volunteers who wanted to help support first responders and assist with recovery efforts. These volunteers included people from local neighborhoods and other states, as well as tourists from foreign countries. The common thread that united them was the belief that they had more than enough to share and the willingness to show their gratitude through volunteerism.

Today Write about an outpouring of support and gratitude you've witnessed that touched you on a deep, human level.

_____

_____

_____

_____

_____

_____

_____

_____

_____

_____

Impeccable Integrity The Buddha's writings teach that a person of integrity is one who has learned to be grateful and harmless (to be kind) in their exchanges with others. This enables them to give with an empathetic heart, be respectful, and know that good will come of it.

Today Write about the gratitude you feel for someone who has given something to you with an empathetic heart, and who asked for nothing in return. That person may have told you that what they'd really given to you was an investment—literally or figuratively—in your future, a way to help you move forward in your life.

_____

_____

_____

_____

_____

_____

_____

_____

_____

_____

Teachers' Impact Teachers appear to us in many different forms. Some may hold formal educational degrees; others may not. However, their lessons enrich the lives of those around them in so many ways. According to the Buddha, the way to honor teachers in your life is to apply their wisdom and pass it on to others.

Today Write about a lesson or two that you've been given and how you're sharing what you've learned with others. Why is that valuable to you?

_____

_____

_____

_____

_____

_____

_____

_____

_____

_____

_____

Homemade Pasta My friend is a master at casually throwing together a fresh pasta dish within minutes. I've watched her make the dough without skipping a beat. As she talks with me, she opens the fridge, chops fresh mushrooms, garlic, and herbs, and, with a few twirls and sprinkles of cheese, dinner is ready in 20 minutes. Delicious!

Today Write about your gratitude for having access to healthy, fresh food and/or the person who makes your dinner.

_____

_____

_____

_____

_____

_____

_____

_____

_____

_____

_____

_____

Humanity

> *"When a person doesn't have gratitude, something*
> *is missing in his or her humanity."*
>
> —Elie Wiesel, 1928–2016, prolific author, professor,
> political activist, Nobel laureate, Holocaust survivor

Today Write about witnessing a lack of care or concern for humanity—a blatant disregard for another person. What can you learn from this experience? Has it caused you to do something differently in your own life?

➤ Even where you see terrible disregard for humanity, a gift may emerge in any number of forms. For one, it may awaken you to an unknown truth or motivate you to take a positive action that you might not have considered before.

_____

_____

_____

_____

_____

_____

_____

_____

_____

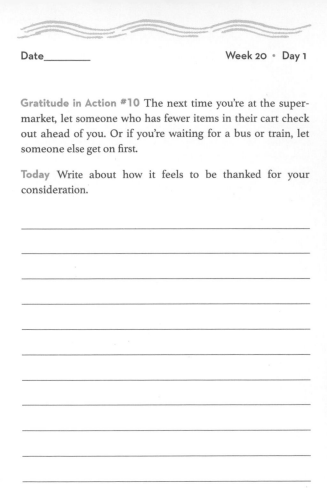

Gratitude in Action #10 The next time you're at the supermarket, let someone who has fewer items in their cart check out ahead of you. Or if you're waiting for a bus or train, let someone else get on first.

Today Write about how it feels to be thanked for your consideration.

_____

_____

_____

_____

_____

_____

_____

_____

_____

_____

_____

_____

_____

Global Connections A study by University of North Carolina at Chapel Hill researchers Sara B. Algoe and Baldwin M. Way found consistent patterns suggesting that the release of oxytocin that occurs during an exchange of gratitude between people is the "glue" that solidifies and binds us into positive, meaningful relationships, including global ones.

Today Write a statement that reflects appreciation for a positive exchange of gratitude beyond your close-knit relationships.

➤ **Your statement of gratitude can relate to an exchange in another part of the world or closer to home, in your own community. Point out how this exchange has improved your life or the lives of others.**

_____

_____

_____

_____

_____

_____

_____

_____

_____

Running a Scenario In his studies, Norwegian psychologist Karl Halvor Teigen found that participants who saw the outcome of pivotal experiences in their lives as positive, compared to what might have potentially occurred (that is, a negative outcome), sometimes considered themselves "lucky."

Today Write about a situation in your life that had a positive outcome, and which could potentially have gone the opposite way. Tap into your emotions of feeling lucky and happy because of the positive result.

_____

_____

_____

_____

_____

_____

_____

_____

_____

_____

_____

_____

_____

Influences Everyone has a slightly different way of expressing gratitude. Contributing factors include cultural values, parenting, and education.

Today Write about the factors that have influenced your view of gratitude. Who or what has influenced you the most and how have you been influenced?

_____

_____

_____

_____

_____

_____

_____

_____

_____

_____

_____

_____

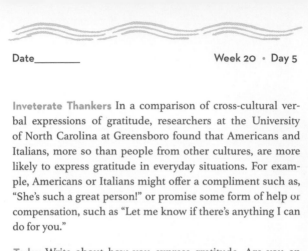

Inveterate Thankers In a comparison of cross-cultural verbal expressions of gratitude, researchers at the University of North Carolina at Greensboro found that Americans and Italians, more so than people from other cultures, are more likely to express gratitude in everyday situations. For example, Americans or Italians might offer a compliment such as, "She's such a great person!" or promise some form of help or compensation, such as "Let me know if there's anything I can do for you."

Today Write about how you express gratitude. Are you an inveterate, verbal thanker?

_____

_____

_____

_____

_____

_____

_____

_____

_____

_____

_____

Awareness of Favor Researchers at the University of North Carolina at Greensboro also observed that people from Iran and Malaysia are more likely than people from other cultures to acknowledge a favor ("You did me a great kindness") or to ask God to reward the person who has been good to them.

Today Write about your experience with expressions of gratitude that may be different from yours.

_____

_____

_____

_____

_____

_____

_____

_____

_____

_____

_____

_____

_____

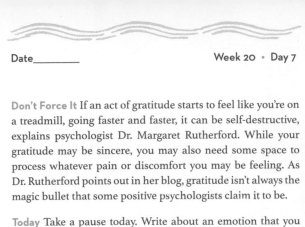

Don't Force It If an act of gratitude starts to feel like you're on a treadmill, going faster and faster, it can be self-destructive, explains psychologist Dr. Margaret Rutherford. While your gratitude may be sincere, you may also need some space to process whatever pain or discomfort you may be feeling. As Dr. Rutherford points out in her blog, gratitude isn't always the magic bullet that some positive psychologists claim it to be.

Today Take a pause today. Write about an emotion that you may need to process.

_____

_____

_____

_____

_____

_____

_____

_____

_____

_____

_____

_____

The Intention of Generosity Generosity can be expressed in many forms: Giving your time, encouragement, wisdom, and money are just a few of them. Everyone has their own way of expressing this virtue.

Today Write your intention for the coming days. It could be: *My intention is to be more generous to those around me. I will start with acknowledging the hard work and dedication of my family.* Feel free to customize your intention statement.

_____

_____

_____

_____

_____

_____

_____

_____

_____

_____

_____

_____

Discounting Yourself Perhaps you didn't succeed at a task because you felt you were unlucky, compared to a colleague who always seems to have luck on their side. This phenomenon is called "comparative concern," a state of mind where you discount any gratitude that could be associated with an outcome, even if it is somewhat positive. In other words, instead of feeling gratitude for your own work, you may be only moderately pleased with it.

Today Write about a time when you engaged in this type of comparison. Even if the outcome of the project wasn't what you'd hoped for, make a list, below, of things you learned or insights you gained about yourself or the project.

_____

_____

_____

_____

_____

_____

_____

_____

_____

_____

Precious Currency

> *"None is more impoverished than the one who has no*
> *gratitude. Gratitude is a currency that we can mint*
> *for ourselves and spend without fear of bankruptcy."*

—Fred De Witt Van Amburgh, 1866–1944, writer and publisher

Today Consider the different ways of expressing gratitude and giving to others that are offered in this journal. Write about the elements of gratitude that you see as potential currency.

_____

_____

_____

_____

_____

_____

_____

_____

_____

_____

_____

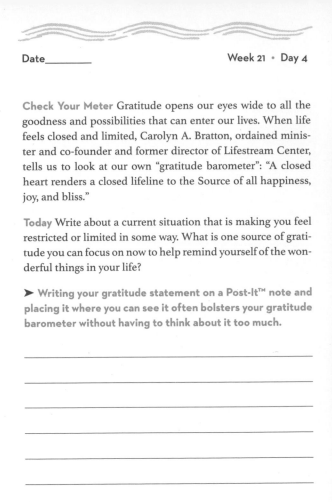

Check Your Meter Gratitude opens our eyes wide to all the goodness and possibilities that can enter our lives. When life feels closed and limited, Carolyn A. Bratton, ordained minister and co-founder and former director of Lifestream Center, tells us to look at our own "gratitude barometer": "A closed heart renders a closed lifeline to the Source of all happiness, joy, and bliss."

Today Write about a current situation that is making you feel restricted or limited in some way. What is one source of gratitude you can focus on now to help remind yourself of the wonderful things in your life?

➤ Writing your gratitude statement on a Post-It™ note and placing it where you can see it often bolsters your gratitude barometer without having to think about it too much.

_____

_____

_____

_____

_____

_____

_____

_____

Motivation Awareness Giving, motivated by the desire to get something back in return, is considered a debt. Kindness and thanks must be a pure transaction without hidden motives.

Today Write about an occasion when you received a kindness, or perhaps offered one to someone else, where there may have been a hidden motive behind the desire to give or receive that kindness. How did that feel?

_____

_____

_____

_____

_____

_____

_____

_____

_____

_____

_____

_____

Take a Look in the Mirror Being kind to ourselves and acknowledging the beauty within us is a form of self-love, self-care, and self-gratitude.

Today Write about an aspect of your personality that you love.

_____

_____

_____

_____

_____

_____

_____

_____

_____

_____

_____

_____

_____

_____

Warm Wishes

"My socks may not match, but my feet are always warm."

—Maureen McCullough, Northeast/Mid-Atlantic
Regional Field Director, Catholic Relief Services

Today Think of a situation that caused you a great deal of stress, perhaps in the last year or so, and write about why you no longer feel that way. How did you make the transition from feeling stressed out to feeling secure, at peace, and full of gratitude?

_____

_____

_____

_____

_____

_____

_____

_____

_____

_____

_____

Gratitude in Action #11 Have you noticed that your GIAs are increasingly starting to move toward expressing kindness, care, and acknowledgment of others in your life? Your GIA practice will continue to focus and expand into meaningful kindness, service, and expressions of awareness of those around you.

Today Write about a simple act of compassion or understanding that you can offer to someone today. What would that look like?

_____

_____

_____

_____

_____

_____

_____

_____

_____

_____

_____

_____

_____

Partnership Nonverbal communication of gratitude in partnerships is often expressed through little gestures and considerate behaviors, other than saying, "I love you."

Today Write about how you can show more gratitude to your partner through kind gestures or considerate behaviors.

_____

_____

_____

_____

_____

_____

_____

_____

_____

_____

_____

_____

_____

_____

A Link to Patience Northeastern University researchers have concluded that the practice of simple gratitude, such as deliberately taking notice of the positive things that happen around you every day, helps to build resilience. When you focus on the good, you gain more patience and self-control.

Today Write about how the benefits of having more patience could enrich your life. Could it make you kinder or more effective—or something else?

_____

_____

_____

_____

_____

_____

_____

_____

_____

_____

_____

Self-Esteem Booster Grateful individuals acknowledge that they have benefited from another person's generosity, which makes them feel valued. This boost in self-esteem contributes to higher levels of psychological well-being.

Today Write about how the generosity of another person has helped you recognize your own value.

_____

_____

_____

_____

_____

_____

_____

_____

_____

_____

_____

_____

_____

Rewiring the Circuits Learning a new habit creates new neurological pathways in your brain. The process involved in making those new connections, as well as removing old ones, is called "neuroplasticity." When you engage in a new habit, such as keeping a gratitude journal, your brain learns to automatically focus on positive experiences, causing your "outlook default" to be one of gratitude. That outlook will occur with increasing ease and speed the longer you reinforce the habit of gratitude.

Today Write about a recent experience when you realized that your first reaction was one of gratitude. Was that *outlook default* surprising to you?

_____

_____

_____

_____

_____

_____

_____

_____

_____

Counting More Blessings Gratitude can foster a feeling of spirituality. Historical studies have shown that there is a connection between gratitude and spirituality in most religions.

Today Write about the connection between gratitude and spirituality in your own life.

_____

_____

_____

_____

_____

_____

_____

_____

_____

_____

_____

_____

_____

Broadening the Scope As a positive emotion, gratitude enhances the brain's ability to be flexible and creatively find solutions that help reduce stress and build resilience.

Today Write about one of your creative solutions that kept a world of stress from crashing down on you.

_____

_____

_____

_____

_____

_____

_____

_____

_____

_____

_____

_____

_____

Gratitude in Action #12 Buy a copy of your favorite book and give it to a friend who will really appreciate it.

Today Write about why you enjoyed reading the book so much and the meaning it may hold for the person who receives it.

_____

_____

_____

_____

_____

_____

_____

_____

_____

_____

_____

_____

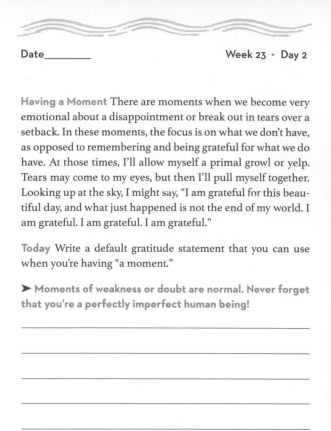

Having a Moment There are moments when we become very emotional about a disappointment or break out in tears over a setback. In these moments, the focus is on what we don't have, as opposed to remembering and being grateful for what we do have. At those times, I'll allow myself a primal growl or yelp. Tears may come to my eyes, but then I'll pull myself together. Looking up at the sky, I might say, "I am grateful for this beautiful day, and what just happened is not the end of my world. I am grateful. I am grateful. I am grateful."

Today Write a default gratitude statement that you can use when you're having "a moment."

➤ **Moments of weakness or doubt are normal. Never forget that you're a perfectly imperfect human being!**

_____

_____

_____

_____

_____

_____

_____

_____

_____

Entitlement Narcissism is the antithesis of gratitude. Gratitude is about giving to others, but narcissism is all about being self-centered and self-absorbed. Clinical psychologist Rebecca Solom offers a clear insight: "Individuals high in narcissism may not even notice that a gift has occurred because they believe they are entitled to the benefit."

Today Write about how you could help someone with narcissistic tendencies to accept a gift, favor, or kindness with gratitude.

➤ You are merely sharing an attitude of gratitude. It is not your job to fix another person's narcissism. However, helping them to identify a generous action, when it happens, might also help them voice an appropriate expression of gratitude.

_____

_____

_____

_____

_____

_____

_____

_____

_____

Harvest Time Wampanoag Prayer

"Let us give thanks to the creator for all that he gives. The harvest moon has shined its brilliance over our home and now as we store the harvest of our work the creator gives his sustenance. The Earth will now rest through the coming seasons, storing the energy needed to once again feed our people."

—Michael "Tender Heart" Markley, author and chairperson, Seaconke-Wampanoag tribe

Today Write about something that your work may have yielded (i.e., your harvest), and which brought you a sense of pride and gratitude.

_____

_____

_____

_____

_____

_____

_____

_____

Revisiting Opportunity Today, continue to reflect on the Wampanoag Prayer. There is a time to rest and wait before taking action again. During this pause, amazing opportunities and helpful people can show up, bringing with them resources, connections, or inspiration.

Today Write about a pause that you may need to take from your career, personal relationships, or another part of your life, and allow the process to flow forward naturally.

➤ **Allowing yourself to take a pause is an important part of being open to letting others contribute to your highest good.**

_____

_____

_____

_____

_____

_____

_____

_____

_____

_____

The Boomerang Effect When I was a kid, my mother told me all the time that withholding forgiveness from my brother, "who was being a pain," was not just a means of punishing him, but it was hurtful to me as well. Sassy as always, I had no problem telling her, "Yeah, well, he doesn't deserve the privilege of my love and presence, because he's a royal pain in the butt!" My mother explained that this line of thinking was hurtful to *both* of us, because it kept us from enjoying each other's company, playing together, and sharing certain things.

The lesson: The gratitude cycle creates a social bond. Holding grudges limits and puts conditions on your willingness to be in the cycle of giving and receiving.

Today Write about an early lesson you learned about the importance of forgiveness.

_____

_____

_____

_____

_____

_____

_____

_____

Incompatible Feelings Envy and gratitude cannot exist at the same time. They are opposing feelings. Gratitude minimizes envy of those who have (or appear to have) more than you.

Today Write about someone you envy or who makes you feel jealous. Is there something positive about that person that makes you feel grateful to know them? How can recognizing that positive attribute help transform your relationship into a more appreciative one?

_____

_____

_____

_____

_____

_____

_____

_____

_____

_____

_____

Gratitude in Action #13 Offer forgiveness.

Today Bring to mind someone who has upset you recently. Write a note of acceptance and forgiveness to them, below. You don't have to actually send the note, unless you care to do so. The act of forgiveness can be remote.

_____

_____

_____

_____

_____

_____

_____

_____

_____

_____

_____

_____

_____

_____

Beyond Ourselves Leading gratitude researcher Robert A. Emmons, PhD, suggests that "humble dependence on others," the recognition that others are a source of goodness outside of ourselves, is a vital component of gratitude. In short, according to Emmons, "Other people . . . help us achieve goodness in our lives."

Today Reflect on how you feel about the concept of *humble dependence on others.*

➤ Knowing that you're willing to give or accept gratitude from others is key to creating a grateful heart.

_____

_____

_____

_____

_____

_____

_____

_____

_____

_____

Dedication to Others There are so many nonverbal ways to express gratitude. For example, an athlete can express gratitude by being a great teammate, and, of course, you can show your gratitude by leading or being part of a team at home or at work.

Today Write about how being a great teammate shows gratitude to those around you.

_____

_____

_____

_____

_____

_____

_____

_____

_____

_____

_____

_____

Wealth

> *"It is only with gratitude that life becomes rich."*
>
> —Dietrich Bonhoeffer, 1906–1945,
> theologian and anti-Nazi dissident

Today Write a gratitude statement about an experience that has enriched, elevated, or enlightened you.

_____

_____

_____

_____

_____

_____

_____

_____

_____

_____

_____

_____

_____

Friends and Neighbors In a recent survey, conducted by the Pew Research Center on the topic of where people find meaning in life, respondents who mentioned friends as a source of meaning rated their life satisfaction 6 percent higher (on a zero-to-10 scale) than those who did not. Contributing factors included having friends who live nearby and considering those friends a part of their extended family, as well as being generally supportive people.

Today Write about the aspects of your friendships that bring you the most joy.

_____

_____

_____

_____

_____

_____

_____

_____

_____

_____

Recognizing the Kindness of Others People who are grateful recognize the kindness of others and accept blame when it is appropriate, rather than blaming others.

Today Write about a time when you accepted responsibility for a misstep that you could have blamed on someone else. Why was it important for you to do this?

_____

_____

_____

_____

_____

_____

_____

_____

_____

_____

_____

_____

Wisdom in Stumbling We may trip, stumble, and fall down at times, but these experiences teach us valuable lessons that help steer our course and make the next experience a better one.

Today Write about a lesson you've learned from a recent setback. Why are you grateful for this lesson?

_____

_____

_____

_____

_____

_____

_____

_____

_____

_____

_____

_____

_____

_____

The Intention of Relationship Appreciation, gratitude, and acknowledgment of the people in our lives requires mindfulness. To take others for granted is to overlook their part in the gratitude cycle, and to disregard what their benevolence brings to you, as well their gratitude for what you bring to them.

Today Write an intention to be more aware of your relationships with others. For example: *My intention for the next few weeks is to be more mindful of my relationships and to notice the things they contribute to my life that make me happy.*

_____

_____

_____

_____

_____

_____

_____

_____

_____

_____

_____

_____

Appreciating Your Own Value

> *"Once you start to recognize the contributions that*
> *other people have made to your life—once you realize*
> *that other people have seen the value in you—you*
> *can transform the way you see yourself."*

—Robert A. Emmons, PhD, psychologist, professor, and
leading expert in the field of scientific research on gratitude

Today Reflect on the positive feedback and appreciation shown
to you by others. How has that feedback increased your belief
in yourself?

_____

_____

_____

_____

_____

_____

_____

_____

_____

_____

_____

Psychological Hurdles Researchers have found that "self-serving bias" can be a hurdle to being grateful: When things go great, we take credit, but when something goes wrong, we may blame others. This bias goes against the principles of gratitude. A grateful person acknowledges all the people who have made things "go great" and who have helped them achieve their goals.

Today Write the names of three people who have helped you reach a goal or realize a dream. What important part did they play in the process?

_____

_____

_____

_____

_____

_____

_____

_____

_____

_____

Being in It Together Being in a meaningful relationship, such as having a spouse or partner, was the first thing that came to mind for one out of five participants in a Pew Research Center survey of life satisfaction. Regardless of their status (age, income, religion, etc.), these individuals rated their life satisfaction (happiness) 9 percent higher than those who didn't mention a partner.

Today Write about how a meaningful, past or present relationship has enriched your well-being and happiness.

➤ We may also have meaningful relationships with someone other than a spouse.

_____

_____

_____

_____

_____

_____

_____

_____

_____

_____

Breathless Moments For several years, I lived and worked in Australia. During that time, I did my best to explore as much as I could while working a full-time job. I'll always remember the moment I stood on the edge of the Great Ocean Road and looked out over the Southern Ocean. I'd never seen anything so breathtaking, and my eyes filled with tears. In that moment I realized how insanely blessed I was to live and work in such a beautiful place.

Today Write about a moment when you realized, in every fiber of your being, that you are blessed beyond your wildest dreams.

_____

_____

_____

_____

_____

_____

_____

_____

_____

Linking in Patience Northeastern University researchers Leah Dickens and David DeSteno have found that the cultivation of patience is a significant by-product of practicing gratitude on a daily basis.

Today Think about this past week: When and in which situation could you have been more patient? Is there any possibility that inserting gratitude into the experience could have helped ease that impatience?

_____

_____

_____

_____

_____

_____

_____

_____

_____

_____

_____

_____

Nurturing Gratitude In studies of adolescent children, researchers have found that boys are less grateful than girls. Boys, however, can gain an awareness of gratitude and develop a gratitude practice if they are given emotional support by their families.

Today Write about the emotional support you received from your family, as you were growing up, and how that fostered an attitude of appreciation and gratitude.

➤ In this gratitude reflection, *family* also includes people other than *biological* members of your family.

_____

_____

_____

_____

_____

_____

_____

_____

_____

_____

_____

Gratitude in Action #14 Play some uplifting music at work—
it might even encourage a dance break for everyone!

Today Can you imagine how much laughter could spin out
of just this short burst of fun? Write about what you would
appreciate about the music and laughter.

_____

_____

_____

_____

_____

_____

_____

_____

_____

_____

_____

_____

_____

Control Freaks Step Aside Embracing gratitude, as part of your lifestyle, sometimes means learning to accept life as it comes and giving up the need to control everything. Gratitude fosters this mantra: *I accept things as they are, imperfect as they may be. I am still grateful for all that I have.*

Today Write out the mantra. Below it, list two or three things you're willing to stop trying to control and accept in this moment.

➤ If the label "control freak" triggers you, try using a humorous version borrowed from a dear friend of mine: "control enthusiast."

_____

_____

_____

_____

_____

_____

_____

_____

_____

_____

Just World Hypothesis As the saying goes, "You get what you deserve." Unfortunately, the "just world hypothesis" perpetuates a feeling of entitlement and disappointment when you don't get what you think you deserve. As Robert A. Emmons, PhD, arguably the world's leading expert on gratitude, notes, "If you deserve everything, if you're entitled to everything, it makes it a lot harder to be grateful for anything."

Today Reflect on when and under what circumstances the just world hypothesis may have cropped up in your life. How has it hindered or overshadowed your ability to appreciate and enjoy even small wins along your journey?

_____

_____

_____

_____

_____

_____

_____

_____

_____

Practicing Acceptance Life is messy and uncomfortable at times, and there will be days when people are just plain rude. When we accept that life is imperfect, we can leave the frustration of needing it to be perfect behind. In that acceptance, we can graduate to feeling grateful for what is good in our world.

Today Write about something you find frustrating and then add a statement of acceptance that may look something like this: *This stuff makes me nuts, and it's definitely imperfect. I will accept it for what it is. Not everyone or everything can be perfect.*

_____

_____

_____

_____

_____

_____

_____

_____

_____

_____

Visual Reminders Scientific research has shown that a daily gratitude routine actually stimulates a region of the brain that is associated with learning, rational thinking, and decision making. These qualities can be helpful in everyday situations, including those at work. Setting a visual reminder on your phone or laptop screen saver to practice gratitude can help keep you on track.

Today Write about a visual cue that you could use to remind yourself to be grateful. What does it look like? Where will you place it?

_____

_____

_____

_____

_____

_____

_____

_____

_____

_____

_____

Contributions to Life Feeling thankful for the contributions that others have made to our lives is based on trust—on freedom from the cynical belief that others may have ulterior motives or nefarious reasons for making those contributions.

Today Write a gratitude statement for a gift, blessing, or intervention that dramatically changed the course of a relationship in your life.

_____

_____

_____

_____

_____

_____

_____

_____

_____

_____

_____

_____

_____

Shifting Focus

> *"When we focus on our gratitude, the tide of*
> *disappointment goes out and the tide of love rushes in."*
>
> —Kristin Armstrong, the most decorated US women's
> cyclist on record and three-time Olympic gold medalist

Today Write about how rediscovering gratitude has helped
you rebound from a disappointment.

_____

_____

_____

_____

_____

_____

_____

_____

_____

_____

_____

_____

Gratitude in Action #15 In the drive-through at Starbucks, treat yourself—and the person behind you—by handing your server an extra fiver to cover their drink or food.

Today Write about what your version of treating another customer at your favorite coffee venue might look like.

_____

_____

_____

_____

_____

_____

_____

_____

_____

_____

_____

_____

_____

Unbridled Joy

> *"I am thankful for laughter, except when*
> *milk comes out of my nose."*
>
> —Woody Allen, Academy Award–winning film
> director, writer, actor, and comedian

Today Write about the last time you laughed out loud with complete abandon. Who or what made you grateful for that pleasure?

_____

_____

_____

_____

_____

_____

_____

_____

_____

_____

_____

_____

Handed-Down Wisdom Our journey isn't just for ourselves; it is meant to be shared with other people to help better their lives. The transfer of wisdom is a time-honored tradition.

Today Write about the wisdom someone shared with you, and which saved you a lot of time, energy, and struggle. Have you shared that wisdom with someone else as well?

_____

_____

_____

_____

_____

_____

_____

_____

_____

_____

_____

_____

_____

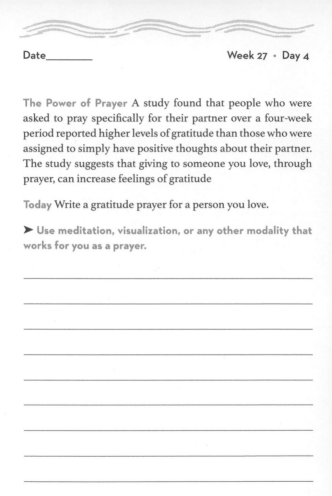

Date_____   Week 27 • Day 4

The Power of Prayer A study found that people who were asked to pray specifically for their partner over a four-week period reported higher levels of gratitude than those who were assigned to simply have positive thoughts about their partner. The study suggests that giving to someone you love, through prayer, can increase feelings of gratitude

Today Write a gratitude prayer for a person you love.

➤ **Use meditation, visualization, or any other modality that works for you as a prayer.**

_____

_____

_____

_____

_____

_____

_____

_____

_____

_____

_____

Connecting Buddhist teacher and author Jack Kornfield was
quoted in the *Huffington Post* as saying, "In certain temples that
I've been to, there's actually a prayer that you make asking for
difficulties: *May I be given the appropriate difficulties so that my
heart can truly open with compassion.* Imagine asking for that."

I cannot imagine asking for difficulties, but I do accept that
learning to be grateful, even in challenging times, is all about
growing from the experience.

Today Write about an important lesson that opened your
heart or helped increase your compassion for another person.

_____

_____

_____

_____

_____

_____

_____

_____

_____

_____

_____

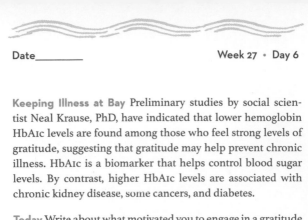

Keeping Illness at Bay Preliminary studies by social scientist Neal Krause, PhD, have indicated that lower hemoglobin HbA1c levels are found among those who feel strong levels of gratitude, suggesting that gratitude may help prevent chronic illness. HbA1c is a biomarker that helps control blood sugar levels. By contrast, higher HbA1c levels are associated with chronic kidney disease, some cancers, and diabetes.

Today Write about what motivated you to engage in a gratitude practice. Why is it important to you and how has it changed since you began?

_____

_____

_____

_____

_____

_____

_____

_____

_____

_____

_____

Turning the Tables A study conducted by psychologist Jo-Ann Tsang, PhD, and her colleagues, indicates that materialistic people have a low level of satisfaction with their lives, and find it difficult to be grateful for what they do have. Consequently, Dr. Tsang and her colleagues concluded that a lack of gratitude contributes to lower life satisfaction.

Today Take an internal inventory and write about the level of your gratitude for having enough versus not having enough. How does this affect your satisfaction with life?

➤ Consider making the Intention of Enough—Week 13, Day 1—the subject of your journal entry today, if that feels appropriate.

_____

_____

_____

_____

_____

_____

_____

_____

_____

Gratitude in Action #16 Give your online community a boost. Using any of your social media accounts, post an image or a meme that focuses on gratitude.

Today Make a short list of ideas for memes or other images that express gratitude and where you might post them online.

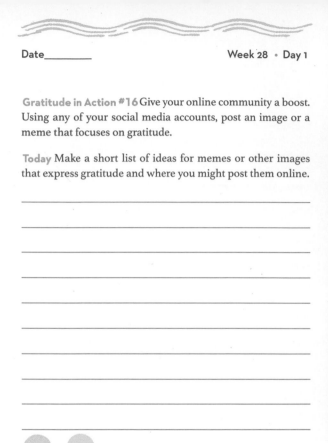

_____

_____

_____

_____

_____

_____

_____

_____

_____

_____

_____

_____

Sage Advice

"When you don't know what you want, it's probably time to begin enjoying what you have."

—Tut.com

Today Write about the three things you're enjoying the most in your life right now.

_____

_____

_____

_____

_____

_____

_____

_____

_____

_____

_____

_____

Stress Relievers Embodying an attitude of appreciation for what is good in your life creates a calming effect and improves relationships.

Today Write about your appreciation for a family member.

_____

_____

_____

_____

_____

_____

_____

_____

_____

_____

_____

_____

_____

_____

Perceptions of Indebtedness

"Feelings of indebtedness related to the obligation to repay the benefactor of a gift lead to lower levels of grateful feelings. This suggests that while one may feel intrinsically motivated to repay the kindness of another by bestowing kindness back on that individual, when one feels an obligation to repay the gift it serves to diminish the view of the good of gifts received."

—Rebecca C. Solom, clinical psychologist

Today Write about a debt that you may have inadvertently placed on a kindness you offered to another person, and how you can relieve them of that debt.

_____

_____

_____

_____

_____

_____

_____

_____

_____

Letting Go of the Outcome The duty of anyone who influences another is to let go of expectations and allow the beneficiary of their influence to explore, choose, and perhaps even reject any of the gifts, wisdom, or direction they've been given.

Today Write about how you felt when the wisdom you offered to another person was ignored, without any expression of gratitude for your insights.

➤ **The gratitude cycle allows free will to be part of the equation. Giving a gift to someone doesn't necessarily mean that they have to accept it.**

_____

_____

_____

_____

_____

_____

_____

_____

_____

_____

_____

Revisiting Relationship Measures Earlier in this journal, we used three statements—called the Expressions of Gratitude in Relationships measure—to evaluate how you show gratitude to your partner. Revisit the three statements, below, and assess your progress using a 5-point scale: 1 (never) to 5 (very frequently):

   * *I express my appreciation for the things that my partner does for me.*

   * *I let my partner know that I value him/her.*

   * *When my partner does something nice for me, I acknowledge it.*

Today Write down your assessment for each statement. Go back to your assessments for these statements on Week 8, Days 4, 5, and 6 to review your growth. How has your sense of gratitude changed and developed?

_____

_____

_____

_____

_____

_____

_____

Tech Reboot What we feed our minds contributes to our mood and perspective for the day. Detoxing from any social media, programs, or other platforms will help remove the temptation to unconsciously start off your day with things that contribute to stress, anxiety about missing out, or fears that you're "not enough." Replace these stressful online engagements inter- actions with more positive ones, such as a gratitude app that appeals to you.

Today Make a list of three to five positive programs or plat- forms that promote gratitude and then explore them.

_____

_____

_____

_____

_____

_____

_____

_____

_____

_____

_____

The Intention of Intuition Everyone has intuition, which can come in the form of a still, small voice inside your head that nudges you to do something. Sometimes, when intuition guides you to help someone else, you may resist acting on it. Author Carolyn Myss suggests that the reluctance to assist another person may be the result of subconsciously viewing that person as a competitor.

Today Write a statement about how you intend to use your intuition—or you can use this one: *My intention is to listen to my intuition more and take action when I do, even if it means helping or thanking someone I don't want to help or thank—at least once.*

➤ Consider the visceral reaction, which you may have had, to the idea that reluctance to help someone else might have something to do with feeling competitive.

_____

_____

_____

_____

_____

_____

_____

_____

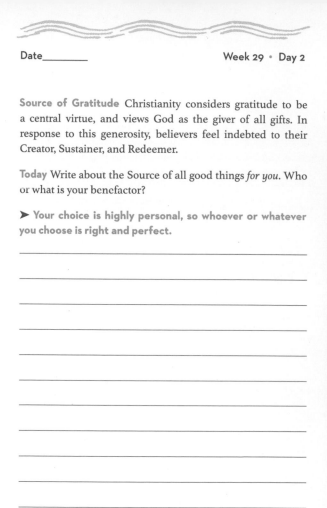

Source of Gratitude Christianity considers gratitude to be a central virtue, and views God as the giver of all gifts. In response to this generosity, believers feel indebted to their Creator, Sustainer, and Redeemer.

Today Write about the Source of all good things *for you*. Who or what is your benefactor?

➤ Your choice is highly personal, so whoever or whatever you choose is right and perfect.

_____

_____

_____

_____

_____

_____

_____

_____

_____

_____

_____

_____

Timed Release It takes time for gratitude to have a positive effect on mental health. Gratitude is like a timed-release capsule, delivering small doses that build up over time, slowly and without disruption.

Today Consider the timed-release nature of gratitude. A few days ago I asked you to write about any changes in your mental health that might have occurred over the past 12 weeks or so. Today, write about any new changes that may have cropped up since then.

_____

_____

_____

_____

_____

_____

_____

_____

_____

_____

_____

Happiness Domino Studies have shown that our everyday interactions with other people are definitely contagious, including those that bring us happiness. We positively or negatively affect one another. Nicholas Christakis, researcher and professor at Harvard Medical School, adds, "... the effect goes well beyond the people with whom we have direct contact. When one person becomes happy, the effect can spread by three degrees, which includes friends of friends."

Today Write about an event that you may have witnessed at work or at home, where happiness had a domino effect.

_____

_____

_____

_____

_____

_____

_____

_____

_____

_____

Synchronicities Countless stories support the belief that the more willing a person is to be grateful for the small things in life, the more frequently those small things just seem to show up. Gratitude and the willingness to relax enough to allow life to surprise you are the keys to happiness.

Today Write about the last time a big or small surprise made you incredibly happy and grateful.

_____

_____

_____

_____

_____

_____

_____

_____

_____

_____

_____

_____

Golf-Course Gift When asked about a recent gift that delighted and filled her with gratitude, award-winning author Angie Mattson Stegall responded with this story: "Walking the greenway yesterday with my husband, I hear a sound. 'Hoot hoot!' I heard it again. Two owls were having a rollicking, clacking, hooting conversation with each other in the trees. Then one of the owls flew across the greenway over our heads. It was MAGIC."

Today Write about a recent magical, unexpected moment that brought you delight and gratitude.

_____

_____

_____

_____

_____

_____

_____

_____

_____

_____

_____

You Are Not a Burden *"I'm so sorry to ask for help"; "I don't mean to bother you but . . ."; "I'm such a mess. I'm so sorry you had to wait for me to pass through this door with all my boxes"* are just a few examples of apologies people make when they ask or allow someone to help them. Sometimes it may feel like we're being a burden in these scenarios, but it's important to remember that it's okay to ask for help when we need it. The gratitude cycle is an exchange of kindness, an expression of empathy, and a willingness to help others, which, in turn, motivates others to do the same.

Today Consider the last time you felt like you were a burden because you asked for assistance. Where did that belief come from?

_____

_____

_____

_____

_____

_____

_____

_____

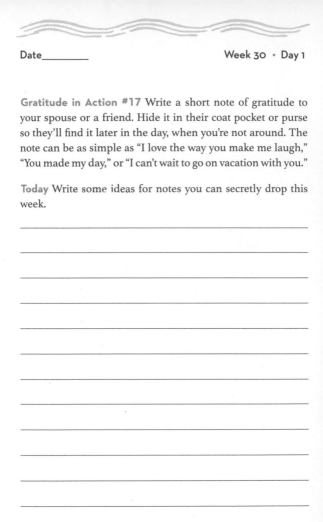

Gratitude in Action #17 Write a short note of gratitude to your spouse or a friend. Hide it in their coat pocket or purse so they'll find it later in the day, when you're not around. The note can be as simple as "I love the way you make me laugh," "You made my day," or "I can't wait to go on vacation with you."

Today Write some ideas for notes you can secretly drop this week.

_____

_____

_____

_____

_____

_____

_____

_____

_____

_____

_____

_____

Pangs or Heart Tugs Keeping track of your intuitive hits is a great way to recognize how often your intuition is kicking in. Those hits, pangs, or tugs at your heart guide you to do or say something you hadn't planned.

Today Make a list of intuitive hits that have impacted you positively in the past 48 hours. For example, did you take a different route on your way to work because something just told you to do so? Perhaps that move shaved 15 minutes off your commute so you had time to grab a much-needed cup of coffee before going into the office.

_____

_____

_____

_____

_____

_____

_____

_____

_____

_____

Positive Thinking

"Years ago I had a Buddhist teacher in Thailand who would remind his students that there was always something to be thankful for. He'd say 'Let us rise up and be thankful, for if we didn't learn a lot today, at least we learned a little, and if we didn't learn a little, at least we didn't get sick, and if we got sick, at least we didn't die; so, let us all be thankful.'"

—Leo Buscaglia, author of *Born to Love: Reflections on Loving*

Today Write about something you learned in the past 24 hours.

_____

_____

_____

_____

_____

_____

_____

_____

_____

_____

_____

The Fear Connection Stress is often the precursor to fear. Barbara L. Fredrickson, professor of psychology at the University of North Carolina at Chapel Hill, has found that maintaining a positive outlook, even when it's challenging, helps to *undo* a negative emotional state. Positive states, such as joy, amusement, happiness, serenity, inspiration, and gratitude, produce stress-relieving emotions.

Today Write about a fear that you would like to undo. Make two columns: In the left column, write down whatever it is that you fear; in the right column, write about any positive aspects of the thing you fear. For example: *I've realized that I can do this differently, and here's how. Or, Even though this situation has ended our relationship, I am relieved and even happy, if I truly admit it to myself.*

_____

_____

_____

_____

_____

_____

_____

_____

_____

Music Trigger Dopamine is called the "happiness hormone." One way to facilitate the release of dopamine is to listen to uplifting music. If the music makes you dance, even better!

Today Jot down the name of your favorite music, album, or playlist below, and write about why it makes you so happy and grateful whenever you listen to it.

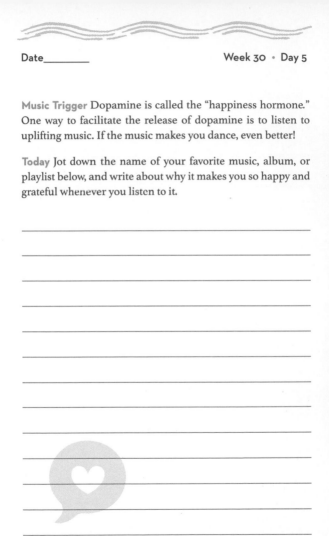

_____

_____

_____

_____

_____

_____

_____

_____

_____

_____

_____

One or the Other Luckily, our brains can't focus on both positive and negative thoughts at the same time. A regular practice of gratitude allows us to retrain our brains to seek out only good things that will enhance our lives by reducing fear, anxiety, and apprehension.

Today Write a gratitude statement about the last time you stopped a negative thought in its tracks, focused on something good in your life, and shifted your thinking.

➤ It is OK to be sad, disappointed, or stressed at times. The objective is not to block out these real emotions, but to offer a way to overcome a negative habit of despair and discouragement.

_____

_____

_____

_____

_____

_____

_____

_____

Opportunity

> *"Gratitude opens the door to the power, the*
> *wisdom, the creativity of the universe. You*
> *open the door through gratitude."*

—Deepak Chopra, author and internationally
known advocate of alternative medicine

Today Write about a positive shift that you may be experiencing creatively or within your own awareness of patterns and habits as a result of your gratitude practice. What have you changed?

➤ Think about where you were 30 weeks ago and compare it to how you view your life today.

_____

_____

_____

_____

_____

_____

_____

_____

Gratitude in Action #18 Offer to help with a chore or task that neither your children nor your coworkers want to do.

Today Write about what that chore or task might be. Consider what it might mean to that person to have your offer of assistance.

_____

_____

_____

_____

_____

_____

_____

_____

_____

_____

_____

_____

_____

_____

_____

Heartfelt Gratitude Kindness and gratitude go hand in hand. Consider the following elements that make gratitude truly heartfelt:

* *There is a benefit to be gained from another person's actions.*

* *You trust that the motives behind those actions are genuine.*

* *You are aware that the other person has gone out of their way to provide a benefit to you.*

Today Write about a heartfelt gratitude that checks all the boxes above.

_____

_____

_____

_____

_____

_____

_____

_____

_____

_____

Reassessing Value The words "I want, I want" typify a state of dissatisfaction. A state of gratitude, on the other hand, sounds like "I am grateful for what I have," explains Piero Ferrucci, psychotherapist, philosopher, and author of *The Power of Kindness.* A grateful mind recognizes the value of what life has to offer, as well as the value of things we might previously have thought of as having no value at all.

Today Write about a shift you may have experienced on the journey to being grateful for something you did not previously cherish.

_____

_____

_____

_____

_____

_____

_____

_____

_____

_____

Intellect Plays a Part In his book *Gratefulness, The Heart of Prayer,* Brother David Steindl-Rast writes that our intellect can help us appreciate a gift when it is offered. Such a gift might be as simple as a piece of wisdom, advice, or simply some time spent together. On occasion, however, our intellect can lead us to overthink a gift and view it as a bribe or a debt with strings attached, Steindl-Rast warns, thus diffusing the positive impact the gift could have had on our lives. The lesson here is to be discerning, not to overthink yourself out of receiving a gift. Receive it with humility instead.

Today Write about a time when your over-rationalized a gift, misinterpreting it as "a debt," only to find out later that the person who offered it had only the best intentions.

_____

_____

_____

_____

_____

_____

_____

_____

Being Spared Intuition can be a warning system that tells you straight from your gut that something is really, really wrong: *Don't go into that room*; *This person is dangerous*; *Something bad is about to happen here, and it's time to leave*, etc. Intuition can serve as a warning that results in a sigh of relief and a feeling of gratitude that you listened to a voice that was too loud to ignore.

Today Write about a situation when you felt you'd been spared from an experience that could have been catastrophic. Acknowledge the emotion of gratitude you experienced at that time, and perhaps still do.

_____

_____

_____

_____

_____

_____

_____

_____

_____

_____

Date_____

Week 31 · Day 6

Social Impact Psychologists who research and analyze differences in conversational styles have discovered that people who engage in deep conversations are happier than people whose conversations are merely superficial.

Today Write about one person with whom you might have a more deeply substantial conversation. What would you share to deepen that connection?

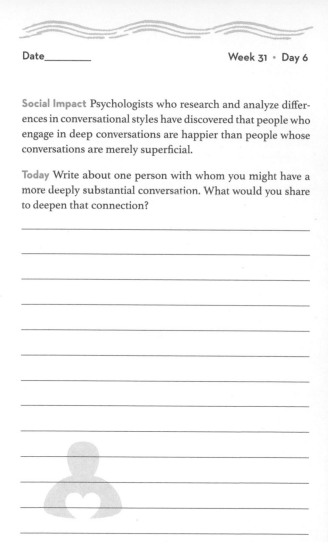

Amplifying Acknowledgment The concepts of gratitude and acknowledgment are intertwined; you can think of them as being on either side of the same coin. And while the language of acknowledgment may include expressions like "*I see you,*" "*I feel you,*" or "*I hear you,*" gratitude amplifies and deepens the power of acknowledgment by saying, "*Not only do I see/hear/feel you, but I thank you as well.*"

Today Think about an acknowledgment you may have offered someone recently. How might you reshape that acknowledgment with an expression of heartfelt gratitude? Write it out.

➤ **The practice of reshaping a prior conversation will make your delivery easier and sound more natural the next time you acknowledge someone.**

_____

_____

_____

_____

_____

_____

_____

_____

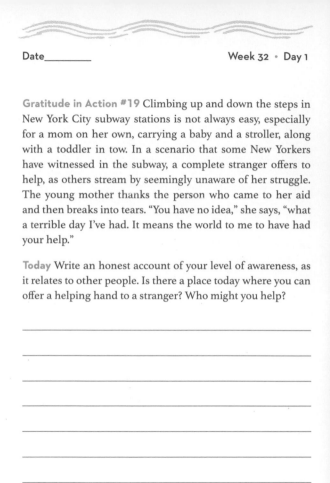

Gratitude in Action #19 Climbing up and down the steps in New York City subway stations is not always easy, especially for a mom on her own, carrying a baby and a stroller, along with a toddler in tow. In a scenario that some New Yorkers have witnessed in the subway, a complete stranger offers to help, as others stream by seemingly unaware of her struggle. The young mother thanks the person who came to her aid and then breaks into tears. "You have no idea," she says, "what a terrible day I've had. It means the world to me to have had your help."

Today Write an honest account of your level of awareness, as it relates to other people. Is there a place today where you can offer a helping hand to a stranger? Who might you help?

_____

_____

_____

_____

_____

_____

_____

_____

Had It Not Happened What would have happened had you not met your current partner or best friend, or had you not jumped on a plane for an adventure that changed your life? What would you have missed out on? Psychologists refer to thoughts like these—appreciating what you have by imagining what your life would be like without it—as "mental subtraction."

Today Write about an amazing experience you would have missed had you not [*insert an experience here*]. For example: *Had I not taken the chance and gone to culinary school in Paris, I would have missed out on having the amazing experience of working with the top pastry chefs in the world.*

_____

_____

_____

_____

_____

_____

_____

_____

_____

Clusters Gratitude is associated with a cluster of related positive words, such as *admiration*, *respect*, *trust*, and *regard*. The word itself is based on the Latin word *gratus*, meaning "thankful." Gratitude, as a state of being, is thought to be on the same emotional level as joy and contentment.

Today Consider the admiration, respect, trust, and regard you may have for another person. Write about why you are thankful for them.

_____

_____

_____

_____

_____

_____

_____

_____

_____

_____

_____

_____

Social Bonds Scientists have found that having gratitude builds social bonds and friendships. Years ago, the company I was working for went through a very challenging merger. Through it all, the vice president, to whom I reported, treated everyone with dignity and respect. We were all so grateful for her kindness. I've always admired this woman and today, many years later, I am proud to still call her a dear friend.

Today Write about a person with whom you may have forged a strong bond out of the kindness and gratitude you've experienced from or given to them.

_____

_____

_____

_____

_____

_____

_____

_____

_____

_____

Generosity Check-in Do you recognize the people and events that have contributed positively to your life? Do you give them credit for being instrumental in contributing to your happiness or success?

Today Write a gratitude statement for the generosity that someone has recently extended to you.

➤ **Remember: Generous people are conduits through which value is added to your life and, by extension, the world around you.**

_____

_____

_____

_____

_____

_____

_____

_____

_____

_____

Mindfulness Meditation and visualization are tools that quiet the mind and help you tap into the deeply intuitive part of yourself. The same tools can also be a means of gaining insight into your day or a particular situation in which you find yourself. Take three minutes to quiet your mind. Breathe deeply and listen to yourself.

Today Write about any insights or solutions that may have come from quieting your mind in the last three minutes. If an insight comes to you later in the day, write it down immediately, and then be sure to say, "Thank you."

_____

_____

_____

_____

_____

_____

_____

_____

_____

_____

_____

Another perspective Transcendent gratitude is another iteration of gratitude, the result of feeling a benefit that comes from a source outside of yourself or other people. An example of this could be gratitude for simply being alive, thankfulness for an opportunity, or feeling blessed to be in a particular place.

Today Write a transcendent gratitude statement. Take note if it's easier for you to access transcendent gratitude or gratitude for a specific person, gift, or favor.

_____

_____

_____

_____

_____

_____

_____

_____

_____

_____

_____

_____

The Intention of Acceptance Samantha Sutton, PhD, life engineer and career and executive coach, uses the list below as a gratitude inventory to determine levels of acceptance. She asks her clients if they can wholeheartedly agree with each statement.

* *I am grateful for exactly where I am today.*

* *I am grateful for my past, because it has gotten me where I am today.*

* *I am grateful for my future, because I know it will be fantastic.*

Today Write an intention statement based on acceptance or use this one: *My intention for today is to be grateful for all that I have and all that I've learned from my past, and I trust that my future will be bright.*

_____

_____

_____

_____

_____

_____

_____

Establishing a Habit Researchers have found that gratitude has long been considered one of life's greatest virtues. Virtues are taught, modeled, and reinforced on a consistent basis until they become a habit.

Today Write about how gratitude has, or has not, been modeled for you.

_____

_____

_____

_____

_____

_____

_____

_____

_____

_____

_____

_____

_____

An Ingrained Memory

> *"Gratitude, as it were, is the moral memory*
> *of humankind. In this respect, it differs from*
> *faithfulness by being more practical and impulsive:*
> *although it may remain, of course, something purely*
> *internal, it may yet engender new actions."*

—Georg Simmel, 1858–1918, German
sociologist, philosopher, and critic

Today Write about an ingrained memory of something for which you have been grateful your entire life.

_____

_____

_____

_____

_____

_____

_____

_____

_____

_____

Taking Notice Using positive psychologist Martin Seligman's "Three Good Things" method (see Week 1, Day 4), focus on a specific moment today that made you feel as if someone really saw your big heart, gifts, talents, or ability to make others smile.

Today Write about three things today that made you feel as if you'd be truly seen or recognized.

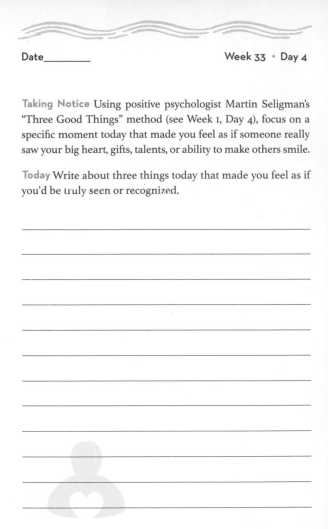

_____

_____

_____

_____

_____

_____

_____

_____

_____

_____

_____

_____

Brain Training A gratitude practice trains the brain to be more conscious of all that is positive in life and fosters an awareness of the positive impact you can have on others. Positives add up to more gratitude and appreciation.

Today Consider some of the positive things that you can offer, or have already offered, to those around you. Make a quick list below. Review the list and put a star next to the things that feel brand-new to you, because you hadn't realized, until now, just how powerful an influence they can have on others.

_____

_____

_____

_____

_____

_____

_____

_____

_____

_____

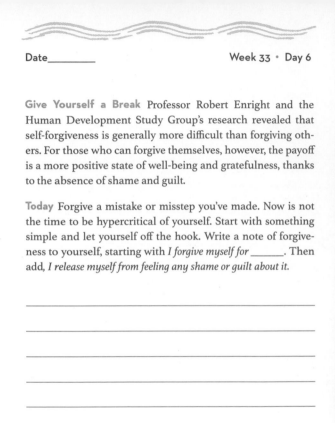

Give Yourself a Break Professor Robert Enright and the Human Development Study Group's research revealed that self-forgiveness is generally more difficult than forgiving others. For those who can forgive themselves, however, the payoff is a more positive state of well-being and gratefulness, thanks to the absence of shame and guilt.

Today Forgive a mistake or misstep you've made. Now is not the time to be hypercritical of yourself. Start with something simple and let yourself off the hook. Write a note of forgiveness to yourself, starting with *I forgive myself for _____*. Then add, *I release myself from feeling any shame or guilt about it*.

_____

_____

_____

_____

_____

_____

_____

_____

_____

The Unseen

> *"The biggest disease today is . . . the feeling of*
> *being unwanted, uncared for and deserted by*
> *everybody. The greatest evil is the lack of love and*
> *charity, the terrible indifference towards one's*
> *neighbor who lives at the roadside, assaulted by*
> *exploitation, corruption, poverty and disease."*

—Mother Teresa of Calcutta, 1910–1997, Catholic nun and saint

Today Consider who you might have thought of as you read Mother Teresa's words above. Write about the kindness or compassion you can give that person today.

_____

_____

_____

_____

_____

_____

_____

_____

_____

Gratitude in Action #20 Create a round-robin with your family at the dinner table tonight and ask each person to share one thing (it can be funny, poignant, or even told with a hint of sarcasm) that made them feel grateful that day or earlier in the week. Expressing your gratitude out loud activates the parasympathetic nervous system, which increases serotonin, the hormone that produces feelings of peace and calm.

Today Write a short list of instructions for your family or friends to play this game tonight.

➤ Remember the four friends toasting on the beach from Week 17, Day 5? That exercise was just another form of this one. Have fun creating an exchange of gratitude.

_____

_____

_____

_____

_____

_____

_____

_____

Roadblocks

> *"Of all the crimes human creatures are capable of*
> *committing, the most horrid and unnatural is ingratitude."*
>
> —David Hume, 1711–1776, Scottish philosopher,
> economist, historian, and essayist

Ingratitude is commonly associated with narcissism, excessive self-importance, arrogance, vanity, entitlement, and an almost desperate need for admiration or validation.

Today Without judgment, write about seeing traits of ingratitude in someone you know. Where do they fall short in expressing gratitude? Do you need to be more conscious of any traits that may be blocking your own expression of gratitude?

_____

_____

_____

_____

_____

_____

_____

_____

Drawing Good to Yourself The practice of praying daily to thank and praise God for bestowing abundance and grace on the believer is a pillar of Islamic faith.

Today Write a gratitude statement for the last paycheck you received.

➤ **Even if you didn't receive exactly the amount you wanted, continuing to acknowledge and be grateful for what you *have* received is what it's all about.**

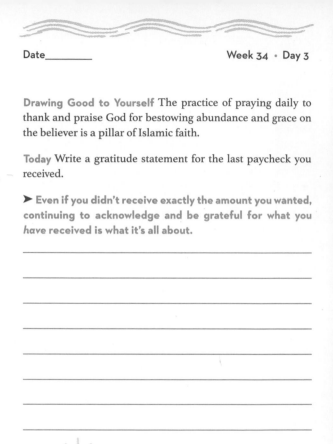

_____

_____

_____

_____

_____

_____

_____

_____

_____

_____

_____

Charitable Activity Using MRI (magnetic resonance imaging), Christina Karns, a neuroscientist and researcher at the University of Oregon, has explored the connections in the brain that support gratitude and altruism. Her study compared what happened in the brain when participants received money in their own accounts as opposed to seeing a transfer of money to a charity. Neurological feedback from the frontal lobe showed that participants responded more positively to "charity-gain" than to "self-gain." Additionally, participants who practiced gratitude regularly registered even higher on a "pure altruism" scale.

The upshot of the study: The more you give, the more the brain views giving as a favorable and worthwhile activity.

Today Conduct your own informal research on this topic. Does it make you feel better to give than to receive? If so, in what way do you feel better?

_____

_____

_____

_____

_____

_____

_____

The Continuum Georg Simmel, a German sociologist, philosopher, and critic (1858–1918), described gratitude as a continuance of memories of either giving or receiving gratitude that live on in our minds and souls as templates for future new exchanges of gratitude. Furthermore, Simmel believed that if these experiences were to be erased, society would unravel, as we are truly held together by a continuum of gratitude, which Simmel considered "one of the most powerful binding agents of society."

Today Write about a continuum of gratitude in your own life.

_____

_____

_____

_____

_____

_____

_____

_____

_____

_____

_____

Ending the Struggle

> *"The struggle ends when gratitude begins."*

—Neale Donald Walsch, author of the series
Conversations with God, and screenwriter for *The Last Avatar* and *Indigo*, among others

Today Think about a time when you decided to let go of a belief or opinion that was negatively impacting you or others. Write a gratitude statement for this experience.

_____

_____

_____

_____

_____

_____

_____

_____

_____

_____

Blandness Imagine a world where everything and everyone were the same: only one kind of music, one food, one fragrance, one book, and one way to speak. Life would be pretty bland, not to mention boring! Celebrating what we appreciate about other cultures, and why we are grateful for them, is an expression of acceptance. As you know by now, acceptance is another facet of gratitude.

Today Write about the beautiful aspects of other cultures that make your life richer.

_____

_____

_____

_____

_____

_____

_____

_____

_____

_____

Gratitude in Action #21 As you'll recall from Week 33, Day 7, Mother Teresa talks about the people who are unseen. Consider someone who seems to be on the outside or fringe of your current circle of friends, family, colleagues, and acquaintances. Acknowledging that person will let them know that they are not invisible.

Today Write about someone who may be a bit on the quiet or shy side. What kind words, praise, encouragement, or thanks could you offer them?

➤ **Be gentle and subtle.**

_____

_____

_____

_____

_____

_____

_____

_____

_____

_____

Cleaning the Lens

> *"Gratitude doesn't change the scenery. It*
> *merely washes clean the glass you look*
> *through so you can clearly see the colors."*

—Richelle E. Goodrich, author, novelist, and poet

Today Write a gratitude statement for being able to change the way you look at something or someone. Think about seeing something from another person's point of view.

_____

_____

_____

_____

_____

_____

_____

_____

_____

_____

_____

Support in the Workplace Studies have found that employees who feel supported by the organization they work for are more inclined to behave in ways that are beneficial to that organization.

Today Write about how you give back to your workplace or other organizations that support you.

_____

_____

_____

_____

_____

_____

_____

_____

_____

_____

_____

_____

Balancing Sadness with Gratitude

> "... Along with [the] sadness we feel a powerful gratitude
> for what is. We cry, but also, we can see the beauty of
> what is, even in the midst of suffering. Where there is
> this true sense of what the world actually is, a vision we
> have of belonging, a felt sense of it, there is always mixed
> in with the sadness of suffering a wide calm feeling. And
> there can even be joy as well, perhaps the purest sort
> of joy, as we recognize the preciousness of life, and its
> utter gratuity: life is present in us and all around us."
>
> —Zoketsu Norman Fischer, poet, author,
> and Zen Buddhist teacher and priest

Today Reflect on this exquisitely beautiful insight. Write a gratitude statement for the things that make you laugh, feel joy, or fill you with awe.

_____

_____

_____

_____

_____

_____

_____

_____

Chosen Attitude

"I see life as a series of choices. This recognition blesses
me with active faith. I choose to make my choices
positive and life affirming. In the face of depression
and a sense of despair, I find a small action which
I can undertake toward the positive. Recognizing that
my life is a matter both of proportion and perception,
I work consciously to keep gratitude as my chosen
attitude and optimism as the lens through which
I view the world. This is not denial. This is courage."

—Julia Cameron, artist, poet, playwright, filmmaker, and author
of *The Artist's Way, Blessings, Vein of Gold*, and many more

Today Write about what the quote, above, has prompted you
to think and feel. Are you feeling courageous, too?

_____

_____

_____

_____

_____

_____

_____

_____

Honoring Delight

> *"It's a negligence if people don't take the time to honor the things that they take delight in, but more importantly, that they share the things that they take delight in. And if you don't do that, there's a loss there. You have to do it to achieve humanity. You have to share delight."*

—Ross Gay, *The Book of Delights: Essays*

Delight is another way of expressing and sharing gratitude for what you experience every day.

Today Write about something that made you light up and smile recently, knowing that if you had shared that delight, someone else would have enjoyed it just as much as you did.

_____

_____

_____

_____

_____

_____

_____

_____

_____

Body Scan "A simple, fast and effective way to connect with yourself and tap into your inner strength is a body scan," says Laura Federico, a clinical social worker who specializes in self-worth concerns, self-empowerment, and the mind-body connection. In helping women learn about their desires, Federico advises: "Start at your feet and work your way up, paying attention to and acknowledging each part of your body. To turn this into a moment of gratitude, thank each part of your body as you work your way up."

Today Write three specific gratitude statements that emerged as you went through this scanning process.

_____

_____

_____

_____

_____

_____

_____

_____

_____

Gratitude in Action #22 What are your favorite flowers? Buy some this week—just one flower or a whole bouquet—as a way of expressing gratitude for yourself.

Today Write about the feelings and memories that come to mind when you think about the flowers you bought. What inspired you to choose them?

_____

_____

_____

_____

_____

_____

_____

_____

_____

_____

_____

Alphabet City On your smartphone, set up a document with the letters of the alphabet listed in a column, starting with A, B, C, etc. On days when you don't feel grateful for anything in particular, reach for your phone and write a note of gratitude relating to each letter (three at a time is sufficient).

Today Start your list below, with an entry for "A." For example, A—I'm grateful for the delicious *apple* I ate this morning. B—I am grateful that my *brown* hair looks great despite the humidity. C—I am grateful for my patient friend *Connie*.

_____

_____

_____

_____

_____

_____

_____

_____

_____

_____

A Human Tapestry

> *"We all should know that diversity makes for a rich*
> *tapestry, and that we must understand that all the*
> *threads of the tapestry are equal in value no matter what*
> *their color. In diversity there is strength and beauty."*

—Maya Angelou, 1928–2014, American poet,
author, and civil rights activist

Today Write about a takeaway from this quote that is especially poignant for you at this time.

_____

_____

_____

_____

_____

_____

_____

_____

_____

_____

Live Longer Studies on well-being, conducted by psychologists Dr. Yoichi Chida and Andrew D. Steptoe, PhD, found a connection between happiness and increased longevity. Their research showed that positive attributes, such as gratitude, joy, happiness, energy, optimism, and a sense of humor, promote life satisfaction and lower mortality rates.

Today Write about the positive side effects of happiness that you may have experienced recently.

_____

_____

_____

_____

_____

_____

_____

_____

_____

_____

_____

A Quick Turnaround How long does it take to turn around negative thoughts, grievances, and frustrations? Researchers have found that the positive effects of gratitude, that is, acknowledging the good around you, can kick in after a very short period—0.5 seconds to 30 minutes. It could be as simple as remembering a cherished childhood pet, comforting cuddles from a parent, or the delight of being in a very special place.

Today Under the heading *When I'm totally frustrated or annoyed, I will remember these good things*, list three things that make you feel happy. Dog-ear this page, so you can find it whenever you need it.

_____

_____

_____

_____

_____

_____

_____

_____

_____

_____

Social Impact Joy is a result of a behavior or action; hope is considered a projection of what is to come. Gratitude, researchers theorize, is a much deeper social emotion than either joy or hope.

Today Write about how witnessing others express gratitude impacts you and those around you.

_____

_____

_____

_____

_____

_____

_____

_____

_____

_____

_____

_____

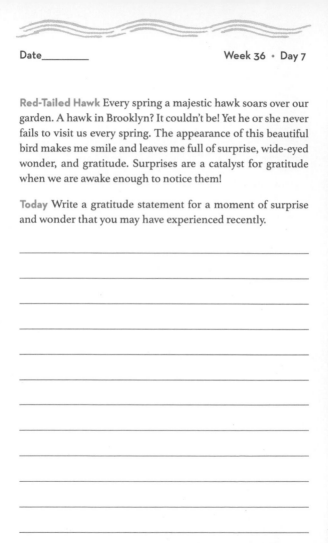

Red-Tailed Hawk Every spring a majestic hawk soars over our garden. A hawk in Brooklyn? It couldn't be! Yet he or she never fails to visit us every spring. The appearance of this beautiful bird makes me smile and leaves me full of surprise, wide-eyed wonder, and gratitude. Surprises are a catalyst for gratitude when we are awake enough to notice them!

Today Write a gratitude statement for a moment of surprise and wonder that you may have experienced recently.

_____

_____

_____

_____

_____

_____

_____

_____

_____

_____

_____

The Intention of Clearing Set the intention to clear out physical or emotional things that you no longer need in your life. Getting bogged down in old energy creates stagnation and distracts you from letting goodness come into your life. Donating things like sheets, towels, and extra pots and pans to a community center can help support many people. Clearing out your home brings in fresh energy, and space literally opens up around you.

Today Set an intention to clear out an area of your life and write about why you've chosen it. As you consider the items you intend to let go of, also write a gratitude statement for how those things have served you well in the past. For instance: *I am so grateful for these shoes I am giving away; I have had so many good times with friends when I wore them.*

_____

_____

_____

_____

_____

_____

_____

_____

Aspects of Trust A concept we've touched on a few times before in this journal is "pure intention," which occurs when you give to another person without expecting anything in return. The exchange requires trust, discernment, and the mutual understanding that nothing is owed and there is no debt to repay.

Today Write about the trust you had in the last person who did a favor for you or gave you a gift. How did you know that their intention to give was pure and they wouldn't "hold it over your head"?

_____

_____

_____

_____

_____

_____

_____

_____

_____

_____

The Gift of Being Incomplete Gratitude is not based on courage, strength, or talent: It is a reflection of our willingness to be seen as incomplete. The philosophical underpinning of gratitude is the recognition that we cannot manage everything alone. The acts of giving and receiving are not solo endeavors.

Today Write about the degree to which you are willing to acknowledge your incompleteness and allow others to help you.

Three Patterns In *The Gifts of Imperfection*, Brené Brown identifies three key patterns associated with the relationship between joy and gratitude:

* *People who describe their lives as joyful actively practice gratitude every day.*

* *Both joy and gratitude are considered spiritual practices that are underpinned by belief in our human interconnectedness and a power greater than ourselves.*

* *Happiness is considered a human emotion, while joy is seen as a spiritual way of engaging with the world, as a result of practicing gratitude.*

Today Try to describe which emotions you've felt first during times of immense gratitude and joy.

_____

_____

_____

_____

_____

_____

_____

_____

Flexibility and Nimbleness Our bodies are amazing: They are nimble, flexible, and get us everywhere we want to go. No matter what kind of exercise you enjoy, show some gratitude to your body for making it possible!

Today Write three things about your body that make you grateful for the exercise it allows you to do.

_____

_____

_____

_____

_____

_____

_____

_____

_____

_____

_____

Boundaries Setting clear boundaries is a means of ensuring that relationships are mutually respectful and supportive. The boundaries we set in our relationships are also a reflection of our self-esteem.

Today Write a gratitude statement for a boundary you set recently and why it was important for you to set that boundary.

_____

_____

_____

_____

_____

_____

_____

_____

_____

_____

_____

_____

_____

_____

JOMO During "Oprah's 2020 Vision: Your Life in Focus" tour, Oprah Winfrey proclaimed that she is all about JOMO—the joy of missing out; that is, consciously disconnecting and living life offline. Winfrey described her delight at being at home and reading on her deck or enjoying the company of other people.

Today Write about what JOMO might look like for you, if you weren't distracted by various devices and social media.

_____

_____

_____

_____

_____

_____

_____

_____

_____

_____

_____

Gratitude in Action #23 As a GIA, offer to make a friend their favorite meal. If you're not a cook, take them out for a meal, as your treat, or have it delivered to their home.

Today Write about the person who will receive your Gratitude in Action. What will you make or order for them, and what meaning might that gift hold for them?

_____

_____

_____

_____

_____

_____

_____

_____

_____

_____

_____

_____

Take the Next Exit

> *"I want to say thank you to all the people who walked into my life and made it outstanding, and all the people who walked out of my life and made it fantastic."*
>
> —Anonymous

Today Shedding relationships that no longer work for you is an important aspect of personal growth. Write about how grateful you are to have let go of someone whose exit was particularly important to you.

➤ **Wish that person all the best. Grudges have no place in a grateful heart.**

_____

_____

_____

_____

_____

_____

_____

_____

_____

_____

Less Dread In a study conducted by psychologists Robert A. Emmons and Michael E. McCullough, participants who practiced gratitude felt more optimistic about the upcoming week than nonpractitioners. The study concluded that gratitude leads to less dread and apprehension in daily life and a greater sense of well-being.

Today Write about what feels hopeful and promising about your upcoming week.

_____

_____

_____

_____

_____

_____

_____

_____

_____

_____

_____

Ninety-Day Staying Power The effects of a consistent practice of gratitude may have a lasting effect on your brain. Researchers are on the way to proving that regular expression of gratitude trains the brain to be more sensitive to the experience of gratitude in as little as three months.

Today Write about an aspect of your mental health that has improved over the past few months.

_____

_____

_____

_____

_____

_____

_____

_____

_____

_____

_____

The Altruistic Brain Researchers at the University of Oregon found that people who engage in a regular gratitude practice are more altruistic—and more charitable—than nonpractitioners. This discovery has led them to believe that a gratitude practice orients the brain to feel more rewarded when others benefit from our charity.

Today Write about your own attitude toward altruism. Are you more inclined to donate time, money, or resources to a cause now, compared to 6–12 months ago? If so, can you explain why?

_____

_____

_____

_____

_____

_____

_____

_____

_____

_____

Be in the Moment Our society operates at a speed most of us can't keep up with. Unless we make a conscious effort to live in the moment, we can easily forget our accomplishments, and life passes us by like a speeding train.

Today Take a moment to be in the moment, here and now. Write about three recent achievements or accomplishments that have made you feel particularly proud.

_____

_____

_____

_____

_____

_____

_____

_____

_____

_____

_____

_____

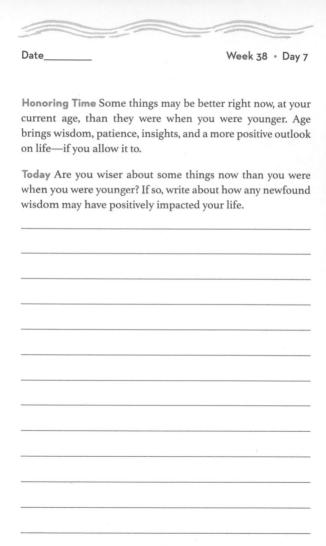

Date_____   Week 38 · Day 7

Honoring Time Some things may be better right now, at your current age, than they were when you were younger. Age brings wisdom, patience, insights, and a more positive outlook on life—if you allow it to.

Today Are you wiser about some things now than you were when you were younger? If so, write about how any newfound wisdom may have positively impacted your life.

_____

_____

_____

_____

_____

_____

_____

_____

_____

_____

_____

_____

_____

Gratitude in Action #24 Creative expression plays a part in our spiritual health and personal vibrancy. It can be expressed in countless ways, from making art and solving complicated math problems to cooking and playing basketball, and the list goes on!

Today Consider the creativity of someone you'd like to support. It could be a child who wants you to color with them, or an adult who may be yearning for a new paintbrush or support for a new project they're about to pitch at work. Write about how you can help. Then do it.

_____

_____

_____

_____

_____

_____

_____

_____

_____

_____

Heartfelt Action Offering forgiveness freely is essential to receiving it freely. In addition, acting in a way that shows that your forgiveness is sincere also has a healing effect on the receiver by defusing any shame or embarrassment they may be feeling.

Today Write about a time when you were able to clear up resentment or hurt feelings with another person. How did resolving the issue change your emotional state?

_____

_____

_____

_____

_____

_____

_____

_____

_____

_____

A Peaceful Mind A study that explored the relationship between gratitude and well-being in daily life showed that participants who practiced gratitude every day got a better night's sleep than participants who did not engage in a regular gratitude practice. Researchers concluded that a better night's sleep stems from the positive by-products of a regular gratitude practice—that is, less dread, fear, and apprehension—and support a more peaceful existence. I used to stress out about deadlines so much that I didn't sleep more than three hours a night for months on end. The insertion of gratitude into my life has dramatically changed my sleep patterns for the better. Now it's just my husband's snoring that keeps me up!

Today Write about your current state of mind. Are you feeling calmer and more peaceful? Which hindrances to sleep have you been able to banish?

_____

_____

_____

_____

_____

_____

_____

Being of Service The Sanskrit spiritual verses, *The Bhagavad Gita*, underscore the importance of helping others: "God is present in every act of service. All life turns on this law . . . Whoever violates it, indulging his sense for his own pleasure and ignoring the needs of others, has wasted his life."

Giving to others is a critical part of the gratitude continuum.

Today Review the journey you've made in the pages of this journal over the last months. How and where have you seen service in the form of kindnesses or compassion to those around you?

_____

_____

_____

_____

_____

_____

_____

_____

_____

_____

Spiritual Support Studies have shown that religion, or a spiritual practice, may help people maintain gratitude even during times of distress. Coping strategies, such as prayer or meditation, create an opportunity to form a strong connection with God.

Today Write about a religious or spiritual practice that grounds you.

_____

_____

_____

_____

_____

_____

_____

_____

_____

_____

_____

_____

Knit One, Purl Two For business culture and development consultant Chrys Sills, knitting is a metaphor for many things in her life, including gratitude: Although flaws may sometimes appear in the knitting, it's "OK," she says, "and I'm accepting of what it is. [At times] I've found myself going back to just before the flaw, pulling back the thread, then starting again, trying something a bit different." The lesson is in the *tink* (*knit* spelled backward); that is, unknitting and taking the risk of going in a different direction in order to create something more beautiful. In the end you're so grateful for having taken the risk.

Today Write about a *tink* lesson. What have you had to undo in order to create something more beautiful in your life?

_____

_____

_____

_____

_____

_____

_____

_____

_____

Calculating the Odds Happiness engineer and author Dr. Ali Binazir has calculated probability data and determined that the odds that you actually exist are almost zero. After all, you are here on a path that began with the odds of your parents meeting (1 in 20,000), multiplied by the odds of their staying together long enough to have children (1 in 2,000), etc. The calculation for the probability of various other events goes on and on. Ultimately, the probability of your being a living, breathing human being comes out to 1 in 102,685,000. That is a 10 followed by 2,685,000 zeros!

I believe your life is worth being grateful for having. Don't you?

Today Write a gratitude statement for all the factors that have put you on your life path. If you can identify events or choices that would have shifted the outcome, include those details.

_____

_____

_____

_____

_____

_____

_____

Gratitude in Action #25 The next time you're in the parking lot outside your local supermarket, offer to return someone else's grocery cart to the store, saving them the trouble of returning it.

Today Write about how it felt the last time someone did a similar favor for you. If they didn't, consider what it might feel like if they had. That's the feeling you're paying forward.

_____

_____

_____

_____

_____

_____

_____

_____

_____

_____

_____

_____

_____

Gratitude Evaluation #1 Psychologist Michael E. McCullough, PhD, and his colleagues, developed *the Gratitude Questionnaire—Six Item Form*, which was designed to measure the level to which we experience gratitude in our daily lives.

For the next few days, score your response—from 1 to 7—to each statement, beginning with the one below. Here's the scoring key: 1 = strongly disagree, 2 = disagree, 3 = slightly disagree, 4 = neutral, 5 = slightly agree, 6 = agree, 7 = strongly agree.

I have so much in life to be thankful for.

Today Using the 1–7 scale, write a number next to the statement, above, that indicates how much you agree with it. Then, below, write about something that makes you feel thankful.

_____

_____

_____

_____

_____

_____

_____

_____

Gratitude Evaluation #2 This Gratitude Evaluation also assesses your general disposition toward gratitude. It is purely subjective.

If I had to list everything I felt grateful for, it would be a very long list.

Today Using the 1–7 scale from Week 40, Day 2, write a number next to the statement, above, and then explain your self-assessment below.

_____

_____

_____

_____

_____

_____

_____

_____

_____

_____

_____

_____

Gratitude Evaluation #3 This evaluation assesses how you see the world around you. It is purely subjective.

When I look at the world, I don't see much to be grateful for.

Today It's OK not to see everything as rainbows and unicorns all the time. Using the 1–7 scale, write a number next to the statement, above, and write below about why you view the world the way you do.

_____

_____

_____

_____

_____

_____

_____

_____

_____

_____

_____

Gratitude Evaluation #4 The findings of Dr. Michael McCullough's research indicate that gratitude creates interdependence; that is, an even exchange between people.

I am grateful to a wide variety of people.

Today Remember to write down your score above on a scale of 1–7, using the scale from Week 40, Day 2. Which individuals have positively affected your choices?

_____

_____

_____

_____

_____

_____

_____

_____

_____

_____

_____

_____

Gratitude Evaluation #5 Gratitude creates social bonds between people.

As I get older, I find myself better able to appreciate the people, events, and situations that have been part of my life history.

Today Remember to give yourself a score on a scale of 1–7 above, and then write a gratitude statement for a specific person, event, or situation that helped shape the person you are today.

_____

_____

_____

_____

_____

_____

_____

_____

_____

_____

_____

Gratitude Evaluation #6 To be mindful is to practice being aware of everything around you. Mindfulness takes practice.

Long stretches of time can go by before I feel grateful to something or someone.

Today Give yourself a score on a scale of 1–7 above, and then write about the things that affect your ability to be mindful.

_____

_____

_____

_____

_____

_____

_____

_____

_____

_____

_____

_____

_____

The Intention of Synchronicity Hermes, one of twelve Olympian gods in Greek mythology, was known for many qualities, including a knack for synchronicity, making it possible for mortals to experience certain events "just in time" and without explanation. A coincidental meeting, a hunch, or simply a feeling can become a significant catalyst for change.

Today Set the intention to be more aware of the synchronistic occurrences around you and how they impact your choices. Write your intention, which can be as simple as this: *My intention is to be more aware of the synchronicity around me and give thanks for it.*

_____

_____

_____

_____

_____

_____

_____

_____

_____

Culture Counts A study of cross-cultural differences focusing on gratitude, led by Todd B. Kashdan, senior scientist at the Center for the Advancement of Well-Being at George Mason University, found that American men associated gratitude with weakness and potential indebtedness, and consequently experienced a low level of grateful feelings. German men, who reported feeling significantly more gratitude than their American counterparts, viewed gratitude as a positive and constructive emotion.

Today Consider the men in your life and write about what you believe their perception of gratitude might be.

_____

_____

_____

_____

_____

_____

_____

_____

_____

_____

Cardiac Patients Various studies have found that patients who experienced heart failure and who kept a gratitude journal for eight weeks, reported that they felt more grateful, slept better, and also detected signs of reduced inflammation.

Today Write a statement of gratitude for something that has positively affected your physical health.

_____

_____

_____

_____

_____

_____

_____

_____

_____

_____

_____

_____

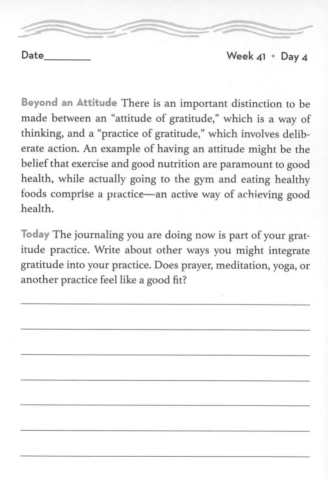

Beyond an Attitude There is an important distinction to be made between an "attitude of gratitude," which is a way of thinking, and a "practice of gratitude," which involves deliberate action. An example of having an attitude might be the belief that exercise and good nutrition are paramount to good health, while actually going to the gym and eating healthy foods comprise a practice—an active way of achieving good health.

Today The journaling you are doing now is part of your gratitude practice. Write about other ways you might integrate gratitude into your practice. Does prayer, meditation, yoga, or another practice feel like a good fit?

_____

_____

_____

_____

_____

_____

_____

_____

_____

_____

Eye Roll All the talk about the wellness perks of gratitude may not seem all that relevant to you today—now that the car seems to have died, the baby just spit up something gray—or maybe green?—and the dog is missing. Yup, it's one of those days.

Today Write a statement of gratitude about your sense of humor and how it gets you through the day. Sarcasm is not just welcome, it's expected, if your day has started like the one described above!

_____

_____

_____

_____

_____

_____

_____

_____

_____

_____

_____

Experiential "Purchases" Cornell University professor, social psychologist, and researcher Thomas Gilovich found that while people enjoy making material purchases, they express more gratitude for experiences such as taking a walk with their child, going on vacation, or sharing a one-of-a-kind experience with family or friends.

Today Write about a simple experience that you still remember with gratitude.

_____

_____

_____

_____

_____

_____

_____

_____

_____

_____

_____

_____

Take a Walk Set aside 20 minutes for a gratitude walk each day. It could be as simple as walking in the parking lot near your workplace or in a park near your home. Vary the locations, if possible. Take notice of every little thing around you—sights, sounds, fragrances, colors, architecture, the way the light hits leaves on the trees, etc. Pause as you notice each element and drink in the moment so that you can consciously register it.

Today Make a list of the things that delighted you on your last walk.

➤ This could be a new gratitude practice for you, if the idea of movement and gratitude resonates with you.

_____

_____

_____

_____

_____

_____

_____

_____

_____

Gratitude in Action #26 Curb any harsh judgment of other people today. Practice observation and acceptance of who they are, at this very moment in time. Remember, we all adapt, grow, and change in our lifetime.

Today Consider the most challenging person you engage with every day. Write about three of their redeeming qualities.

_____

_____

_____

_____

_____

_____

_____

_____

_____

_____

_____

_____

Frequency Illusion Arnold Zwicky, consulting professor of linguistics at Stanford University, describes this complex as a concept or thing that you just found out about, and which suddenly seems to crop up everywhere—like noticing how many red cars there seem to be on the road and then jumping to the conclusion that everyone is driving a red car.

The psychological elements at play in a "frequency illusion":

1. Selective attention—your brain is tickled by a new concept, idea, or thing. You unconsciously keep an eye out for it and, as a result, find it surprisingly often.

2. Confirmation bias—each sighting is proof, reassuring you that the thing, concept, or idea you're "seeing" is now everywhere.

Today Write about a seemingly significant, omnipresent pattern that may have caught your attention recently. Identify why and how this pattern has elicited your gratitude.

_____

_____

_____

_____

_____

_____

Living a Happy Life In a 2017 Pew Research Center Study, researchers found four common elements associated with high levels of life satisfaction: good health, a romantic partner, friends, and a fulfilling career.

Today Write about an element, other than the ones specified above, that contributes to a high level of satisfaction in your life.

_____

_____

_____

_____

_____

_____

_____

_____

_____

_____

_____

_____

_____

Medial Prefrontal Cortex Researchers have found that people who practice gratitude have much greater activity in the learning and decision-making center of the brain, known as the medial prefrontal cortex, as opposed to people who are less grateful, and who experience more activity in areas of the brain that are related to guilt.

Today Write about any feelings of guilt that you may want to be released from.

_____

_____

_____

_____

_____

_____

_____

_____

_____

_____

_____

_____

Carve a New Path One way to strengthen neural pathways in your brain and increase happiness is to consciously perform a gratitude practice or ritual, or engage in some other aspect of the gratitude cycle. As neural pathways become stronger, the likelihood that your brain will have the ability to form new neural connections is much stronger.

Today Write about any changes you may have noticed in yourself or others who regularly engage in a gratitude practice.

_____

_____

_____

_____

_____

_____

_____

_____

_____

_____

_____

_____

Sense Memory More than any other sense linked to memory, smell is the strongest. Every scent you experience passes through both your amygdala (the emotion creation center) and your hippocampus (the stored memory center) before you consciously smell it. For example, the scent of freesia may be a powerful trigger for happy memories of your granny's garden, or the aroma of freshly ground and brewed coffee might remind you of leisurely, pleasurable Sunday mornings spent with your family.

Today Identify a powerful, positive memory trigger that makes you smile. Write a gratitude statement about the memory and the smell that triggered it.

_____

_____

_____

_____

_____

_____

_____

_____

_____

_____

Gratitude Walk Several days ago, in Week 41–Day 7, I suggested taking a gratitude walk for 20 minutes every day, and instructed you to take in everything around you—sights, smells, textures light, other people, etc. How did that go? Where did you walk?

Today Make a list of the things that made you smile and that delighted you on your last walk.

➤ **If you haven't yet had the opportunity to do this exercise, try it out as you walk to work or go to the store today.**

_____

_____

_____

_____

_____

_____

_____

_____

_____

_____

_____

Gratitude in Action #27 To honor the teachers in your community who have had a lasting, positive effect on your life, consider supporting them, either in person or online, with a donation of books or supplies. DonorChoose.org is a good place to start.

Today Write about how you would like to show your gratitude to those who have taught you in the past. Are you thinking of donating money or supplies, or do you have another creative idea in mind?

_____

_____

_____

_____

_____

_____

_____

_____

_____

_____

_____

_____

No Apologies Necessary Do you ever find yourself apologizing when someone holds the door open for you, as you enter a coffee shop, or when you're struggling to balance a pile of books in your arms and open the door at the same time? Instead of apologizing and keeping the focus on you, solution-focused life coach Chelsea Leigh Trescott suggests redirecting the focus to the other person by simply saying, "*Thank you so much.*"

Today Before you say to yourself, "I never apologize like that," take a moment to reflect. Consider a time when you might have apologized, when it wasn't necessary, and write about why you may have felt that an apology was needed.

_____

_____

_____

_____

_____

_____

_____

_____

_____

_____

Cascade Effect Gratitude can foster prosocial behavior (social behavior that benefits another person or groups of people). A single act of prosocial behavior can have a cascade effect, generating new waves of behavior that benefit other people, who, in turn, are motivated to reciprocate an act of kindness, not just to the initial giver, but to others around them as well.

Today Write about an experience where you've witnessed or engaged in the Cascade Effect.

_____

_____

_____

_____

_____

_____

_____

_____

_____

_____

_____

Gratitude: Side A & Side B Christianity makes a distinction between two types of gratitude:

* *Natural gratitude—giving thanks to God for the benefits you've received.*

* *Gracious gratitude—acknowledgment that any goodness bestowed by God is independent of any gifts you may have received from a person or agency other than God.*

Today Write about how your views on natural and gracious gratitude operate within your own belief system.

Better Than Aspirin In the 2003 study, called "Counting Blessings versus Burdens: An Experimental Investigation of Gratitude and Subjective Well-Being in Daily Life," researchers found that participants who regularly dedicated their attention to gratitude, compared to participants who did not focus on a similar practice, reported 16 percent fewer symptoms of physical illness and pain (due to a higher release of dopamine) and a greater willingness to exercise more often and comply with prescribed treatments.

Today Write about any aches and pains that you are no longer experiencing. Oftentimes, we don't notice when the things that have been hurting or troubling us are gone—until we think about it! Add a statement of gratitude for this gift.

_____

_____

_____

_____

_____

_____

_____

_____

Distracted & Confused Social media. Smartphones. Computers. Television. Premium streaming channels. Gaming. As a society, we've become addicted to constant distractions that keep us from being in the here and now. Lack of awareness of what is really going on around us often leads to FOMO, the fear of missing out, instead of focusing in the moment on all the things for which we can be grateful.

Today Write about one to three distractions that you can put on pause for the next 48 hours—and focus on all the blessings and opportunities around you.

_____

_____

_____

_____

_____

_____

_____

_____

_____

_____

Chemical Influencers In her book, *Habits of a Happy Brain*, Loretta Graziano Breuning, PhD, identifies the chemicals that are released when you experience certain emotions. For example, when you experience the joy of finding what you seek, dopamine is at work. When you're experiencing less pain, you can credit endorphins for the release. And for the comforts of social engagement and the pleasure of social importance, you can be thankful for the release, respectively, of oxytocin and serotonin.

Today Write about finding a solution to an issue that has been troubling you. Why is it so important to find one?

➤ **This exercise will start your dopamine flowing!**

_____

_____

_____

_____

_____

_____

_____

_____

Gratitude in Action #28 Leave an anonymous, encouraging note for another customer on the community bulletin board at your gym or the local coffee shop.

Today Using a simple, colorful sticky note or index card, write something like "I'm so proud of you," "You're amazing!" or "Thank you for being such a good person—you made someone's day special!" You are not necessarily leaving the note for anyone in particular. Don't worry: The right person will see it.

_____

_____

_____

_____

_____

_____

_____

_____

_____

_____

_____

_____

Magnetic You Expressing gratitude raises the frequency of your vibrations, creating more positive energy in the world. Daniel T. Peralta, a teacher of metaphysics, explains that gratitude is a magnetic force that draws good things and good people to you.

Today Write about two people you know and compare them. Which one is more negative than the other? Which one is usually more grateful? Which one attracts more opportunities and goodness to him- or herself?

_____

_____

_____

_____

_____

_____

_____

_____

_____

_____

_____

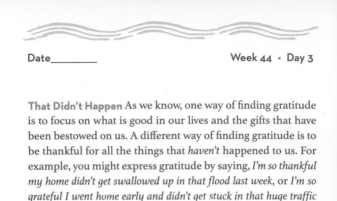

That Didn't Happen As we know, one way of finding gratitude is to focus on what is good in our lives and the gifts that have been bestowed on us. A different way of finding gratitude is to be thankful for all the things that *haven't* happened to us. For example, you might express gratitude by saying, *I'm so thankful my home didn't get swallowed up in that flood last week*, or *I'm so grateful I went home early and didn't get stuck in that huge traffic jam*, etc.

Today Quickly write 10 things you're grateful for that *didn't* happen to you in the past 24 hours.

_____

_____

_____

_____

_____

_____

_____

_____

_____

_____

Four-Leaf Clover Synchronicity, a concept first introduced by psychoanalyst Carl Jung as "meaningful coincidences," can manifest in various ways, including recurring events, names, signs, symbols, and numbers that are particularly significant to you. For example, four-leaf clovers were a special symbol that signified the unique and unexpected love that a friend and her husband shared with each other. When her husband died after a long illness, she kept discovering four-leaf clovers just about everywhere she went. She knew that these sightings weren't random; they were reminders that the love she and her husband had shared still lived on.

Today Write about a synchronistic event or symbol that reminds you of something deeply personal and gratifying in your life.

Eye Contact Making eye contact with someone shows that you're truly present in the conversation. It fulfills the human desire to *be seen*.

Today Write about where and how you can improve the gift of showing others that you've truly seen them. With whom will you make more of a concerted effort to engage in eye contact, or in which aspect of your life will you work toward improving this skill?

_____

_____

_____

_____

_____

_____

_____

_____

_____

_____

Embracing the Distinction At its most extreme, *dependence* is enslavement, as we wait for someone or something to take care of us. *Independence* is alienation, if we don't believe we need anyone. However, *interdependence* is freedom, because it bestows on us the gift of give-and-take. Giving thanks is the best gift we can bestow on another. As Benedictine monk, author, and lecturer Brother David Steindl-Rast views it, the one who says "thank you" is actually saying "We belong together." There is no separation or alienation between the thankful and the thanked; they are one in a continuous cycle.

Today Write about your experience of "We belong together."

_____

_____

_____

_____

_____

_____

_____

_____

All Miracles

> *"Through the eyes of gratitude, everything is a miracle."*
>
> —Mary Anne Davis, Irish social entrepreneur,
> activist, and champion for the rights of children
> and adults with intellectual disabilities

Today Write about an experience that you believe to have been a miracle.

➤ Miracles come in all sizes: small, medium, large, and even supersize.

_____

_____

_____

_____

_____

_____

_____

_____

_____

_____

_____

The Intention of Purpose The process of setting an intention gives you the opportunity to focus on who you want to be and the values you choose to live by, according to business advisor Marla Tabaka. In her view, setting an intention gives you a road map that points you in the right direction to live each day the way you want to live it, along with the purpose, inspiration, and motivation to reach that goal.

If you value gratitude, setting an intention to be kind and helpful to others will help bring that intention to life. Always take an action that aligns with your intention.

Today Write about a value that is dear to you and how you might choose to express that value. You may choose any value and action that speak to you. It is a completely personal choice.

_____

_____

_____

_____

_____

_____

_____

Awestruck Talent It's not hard to see that the pace of working in corporate America is nothing short of insane. One manager at a large multinational team told me that on her early morning walk to the office, before anyone else had arrived, she would have a moment of experiencing wonder and awe, thinking about the people on her team, who were so dedicated. Even to this day, years after working with that team, she hasn't forgotten and never undervalues the gratitude she felt for the talented and creative people with whom she worked, and who were so kind and generous to one another.

Today Write about the things that make you feel grateful for your colleagues or team.

_____

_____

_____

_____

_____

_____

_____

_____

_____

Teaching Gratitude Research conducted by the Greater Good Science Center at the University of California–Berkeley, for the John Templeton Foundation project "Raising Grateful Children," revealed that 85 percent of parents in the study encouraged their children to say, "Thank you," while only 39 percent encouraged them to show gratitude in other ways.

Today Write about one way you can teach a child or another person how to show gratitude.

➤ **Any act of kindness you particularly enjoy will do the trick!**

_____

_____

_____

_____

_____

_____

_____

_____

_____

_____

Happy Contagion A study conducted by Harvard University and the University of California–San Diego found that happiness seems to like company more than misery does. One person's happiness can trigger a chain reaction that has a positive effect on the disposition of their friends, who then pass the joy along to *their* friends, and so on. Happiness is a positive form of contagion that spreads through community networks faster than sadness.

Today Write a gratitude statement for the person whose happiness seems to rub off on you whenever you are together.

_____

_____

_____

_____

_____

_____

_____

_____

_____

_____

_____

Being Enough

> *"The presumption at all times and under all circumstances, should always be that you are good enough, worthy enough, and lovable enough. And that you are exactly the right kind of person, in the right place, at the right time. Otherwise, you wouldn't have been instilled with such dreams in the first place."*

—Mike Dooley, *New York Times* best-selling author of *A Beginner's Guide to the Universe*, *Infinite Possibilities*, and *Life on Earth*; metaphysical teacher; cofounder of Tut.com (The Universe Talks); and creator of "Notes from the Universe"

Today Write a gratitude statement that aligns with the belief that you are "enough."

_____

_____

_____

_____

_____

_____

_____

_____

Transformative Aspect Researchers have found that people who are grateful have low levels of resentment and envy.

Today Identify someone whom you may have envied or resented in the past. Rate your current level of resentment and envy toward that person on a scale of 1 to 5 (1 being low and 5 being high). Write about why those feelings still bother you today.

➤ Your rating on the scale may vary from day to day.

_____

_____

_____

_____

_____

_____

_____

_____

_____

_____

_____

_____

Twenty-one Days Robert A. Emmons, PhD, an expert in the field of gratitude, found that participants in a study, whose age ranged from 8 to 80, and who practiced writing in a gratitude journal for just three weeks, received benefits, such as a stronger physical constitution, a more positive outlook on life, and a greater ability to engage socially with others.

Today Write a statement of gratitude for any physical, emotional, or social benefits you may have gained over the past 21 days. Feel free to scan your journal entries for any patterns that may have emerged.

_____

_____

_____

_____

_____

_____

_____

_____

_____

_____

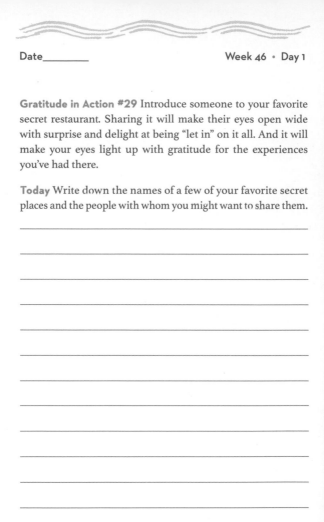

Gratitude in Action #29 Introduce someone to your favorite secret restaurant. Sharing it will make their eyes open wide with surprise and delight at being "let in" on it all. And it will make your eyes light up with gratitude for the experiences you've had there.

Today Write down the names of a few of your favorite secret places and the people with whom you might want to share them.

_____

_____

_____

_____

_____

_____

_____

_____

_____

_____

_____

_____

To Be Seen

"We have to renounce our pride in order to recognize that our happiness depends upon someone else. Many people do not like to feel they are dependent. I knew a man who was unable to receive presents. Whenever anyone gave him something, a book or a tie, he would leave it behind, as if afraid of being in debt. It stopped him not only from enjoying [the gift], but also from opening to another person . . . To be grateful is to let ourselves be known."

—Piero Ferrucci, psychotherapist, philosopher,
and author of *The Power of Kindness*

Today Write about how willing you are to let all aspects of gratitude into your life. Can you allow yourself to be vulnerable and receptive to others?

_____

_____

_____

_____

_____

_____

_____

_____

_____

Full Circle Confidence is about trusting yourself, even at the risk of making yourself vulnerable. The more self-confident you are, the easier it will be to open yourself to others. Vulnerability leads to gratitude. Gratitude ignites joy.

Today Write a gratitude statement about a time when you felt confident and full of joy as a result of trusting in yourself.

_____

_____

_____

_____

_____

_____

_____

_____

_____

_____

_____

_____

Supporting a Cause Researchers at the University of Indiana found that people who are more grateful than others are also more generous when giving to a cause.

Today Write about a cause to which you either donate money or volunteer your time. What fills you with the desire to contribute to the cause? What need is it filling, and what makes you feel grateful for what it is accomplishing in the world?

_____

_____

_____

_____

_____

_____

_____

_____

_____

_____

_____

_____

_____

Genetic Connection The CD38 gene is associated with social bonding; it regulates the release of oxytocin, which is triggered by expressions of gratitude, whether by the giver or the receiver. Research findings suggest that the oxytocin system helps solidify the social "glue" that binds us into meaningful relationships.

Today Write a statement of gratitude for a group of people you are close to, and who regularly express kindness, gratitude, appreciation, and thanks.

_____

_____

_____

_____

_____

_____

_____

_____

_____

_____

_____

_____

Goodness

> *"The roots of all goodness lie in the soil*
> *of appreciation for goodness."*

—His Holiness the 14th Dalai Lama, spiritual leader of Tibet

Today Write a simple statement of gratitude for something you may have perceived as insignificant until now. What impact did it have on you?

_____

_____

_____

_____

_____

_____

_____

_____

_____

_____

_____

_____

_____

_____

Self-Check If you find yourself wanting more, and more, and even more, it's time to check in on yourself. Wanting more—in a context other than normal ambitions—can be a sign of ungratefulness, a powerful indicator that you don't appreciate and give thanks for what you have right now, at this very moment.

Today Write a general assessment of your desire for wanting more. Where in your life do you need to inject a dose of gratitude?

_____

_____

_____

_____

_____

_____

_____

_____

_____

_____

_____

_____

Gratitude in Action #30 While the study of gratitude in institutional settings is relatively limited at this time, some researchers have identified ways to build a workplace culture that promotes gratitude, beyond merely saying thank-you (although they concede that modeling gratitude is important). Their ideas include creating a gratitude board in the staff room, making thank-you postcards that employees can send to one another, giving out gratitude awards, and promoting other activities that identify and recognize the positive and good things in the workplace.

Today Write about one of your own ideas that might help promote a culture of gratitude in your workplace. Who can help you make this happen—and how can it be done?

_____

_____

_____

_____

_____

_____

_____

_____

Social Support For psychologist Robert A. Emmons, PhD, gratitude is a social emotion that provides opportunities for us to strengthen relationships by requiring us to acknowledge how we've been supported by other people and to appreciate the goodness they've brought to our lives.

Today Write about how you may have witnessed or personally experienced social support, as it is described above. How can you improve the social support you offer to others?

_____

_____

_____

_____

_____

_____

_____

_____

_____

_____

_____

_____

Sixth Component of Resilience Psychologists have long believed that there are five components to resilience: social competence, problem-solving, autonomy, forgiveness, and empathy. Now modern research studies have added a sixth component to emotional resilience: gratitude.

Today Write about what makes you flexible, adaptable, and resilient.

_____

_____

_____

_____

_____

_____

_____

_____

_____

_____

_____

_____

_____

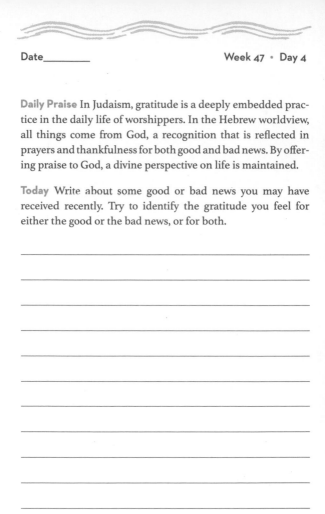

Daily Praise In Judaism, gratitude is a deeply embedded practice in the daily life of worshippers. In the Hebrew worldview, all things come from God, a recognition that is reflected in prayers and thankfulness for both good and bad news. By offering praise to God, a divine perspective on life is maintained.

Today Write about some good or bad news you may have received recently. Try to identify the gratitude you feel for either the good or the bad news, or for both.

_____

_____

_____

_____

_____

_____

_____

_____

_____

_____

_____

_____

Meditate on This Meditation is a practice that uses techniques, such as mindfulness, to reduce stress, control anxiety, promote cognitive health, enhance self-awareness, and lengthen attention span, among other health benefits. As you start each day, use this powerful tool to focus on gratitude.

Today If you haven't already experienced the benefits of meditation, take a moment to make a short list of guided meditation apps that can be downloaded onto your phone. You might want to start with a script from ChangeToChill.org or a guided meditation from the University of California–Berkeley "Greater Good in Action" website.

_____

_____

_____

_____

_____

_____

_____

_____

_____

Happiness Equation Sonja Lyubomirsky, professor of psychology at University of California–Riverside and bestselling author, suggests that there are three primary factors that have an effect on how we experience happiness:

* *50 percent of our happiness is determined by genetics—our personality and temperament.*

* *40 percent is based on intentional activities that bring about well-being and happiness.*

* *10 percent is environmental (or circumstantial), i.e., factors that include the people with whom we surround ourselves and how they encourage our skills and opportunities, our health, income, and religious affiliation, etc.*

A surefire way to achieve happiness is to practice gratitude.

Today Write about elements in your life that bring you the most happiness.

_____

_____

_____

_____

_____

_____

_____

Noticing Growth Human beings are constantly changing: Wisdom deepens as our breadth of knowledge expands, and, as we mature, life experiences influence us to make different choices than those we made when we were younger. All these factors contribute to our growth.

Today Consider someone in your life you've seen change and grow over a period of time. Write about how that growth has become apparent to you. Give yourself bonus points if you email or text that person, telling them how happy or miraculous you believe their growth has been.

➤ Remember, acknowledging and congratulating someone on their progress is also part of the gratitude cycle. Encouragement is a gift.

_____

_____

_____

_____

_____

_____

_____

_____

Gratitude in Action #31 Tell your partner, spouse, or significant other about something they did recently that makes you love them even more.

Today Write a very specific and detailed statement of gratitude, such as *I love that you thought about me today and took the time to plan something special for us to do this weekend.*

_____

_____

_____

_____

_____

_____

_____

_____

_____

_____

The Streets Wandering around the streets of lower Manhattan, taking in the beauty of architecture bathed in exquisite light, makes me feel as if I'm in a world far away. I wonder about the history of the place, the people who once walked the same cobblestone streets, and the lovers who have stolen kisses in the doorways. It makes me laugh and smile to imagine this other world and other people having ordinary experiences in such a beautiful place. In those moments, I am so grateful to live in this amazing city.

Today Write a short story about a place where you've lived or visited that has brought you delight or inspired your gratitude.

_____

_____

_____

_____

_____

_____

_____

_____

_____

Consider All Sides Positive Psychology researchers have found that expressing our gratitude for positive emotions and experiences, both in the present and the past (such as precious childhood memories), makes us happy. They also suggest that building happiness can be accomplished by being grateful for what is to come, i.e., being hopeful and optimistic about the future.

Today Write about how you picture a positive future for yourself. Dig deep and consider what you dream and fantasize about but would never dare share with anyone else.

_____

_____

_____

_____

_____

_____

_____

_____

_____

_____

_____

Exhausted Givers People can sometimes become exhausted givers. Even with every good intention to live in the cycle of gratitude, inevitably there will come a time when you have to say no to a request. Self-care is also part of the gratitude cycle—being grateful to yourself, your abilities, and, yes, even your limitations. There's no need to pile so much onto your plate.

Today Write about a boundary you had to set by saying no, and the gratitude you felt for being able to do so.

_____

_____

_____

_____

_____

_____

_____

_____

_____

_____

Things You Remember We quickly adapt to having new material possessions, but within a short time they often lose their novelty. The shine comes off the penny, so to speak. However, some experiences, no matter how fleeting, live on in our memories and continue to inspire gratitude. I will always remember the chilly July evening, when my husband and I watched the sound and light (*son et lumière*) show at Reims Cathedral in France. It was magical and my deep gratitude for that beautiful experience lives on in my memory.

Today Write about the difference in the level of gratitude you feel for a material item you purchased a few years ago and a wonderful experience you've had. Which one are you still grateful for today?

_____

_____

_____

_____

_____

_____

_____

_____

_____

A Ripple in the Pond

> *"Everything we do for another person has infinite*
> *consequences. Every action gives rise to a ripple effect,*
> *just as a pebble that is tossed into a pond sends out wave*
> *after wave, widening and covering more and more space."*

—Caroline Myss, from *Invisible Acts of Power*

Today Write about a ripple effect that you've experienced, good or bad.

➤ What's important here is to see how, unconsciously, we affect one another.

_____

_____

_____

_____

_____

_____

_____

_____

_____

Selfishness Aside

> *"The value of a man resides in what he gives and not in what he is capable of receiving."*

—Albert Einstein (1879–1955), German-born theoretical physicist who developed the theory of relativity, also known for its influence on the philosophy of science

Today Write about what this quote means to you.

_____

_____

_____

_____

_____

_____

_____

_____

_____

_____

_____

_____

_____

Helping Others Research led by psychologists Robert A. Emmons, PhD, and Michael E. McCullough has illuminated the positive impact that helping or offering emotional support to others has on people who have a grateful outlook on life. In other words, the beneficiary of help is not just the person who receives it; the giver also benefits and is more likely to offer help again.

Today Write about how it felt to lend a hand to another person recently.

➤ If helping another person did—or didn't—make you want to do it again, give yourself bonus points for writing about that.

_____

_____

_____

_____

_____

_____

_____

_____

_____

_____

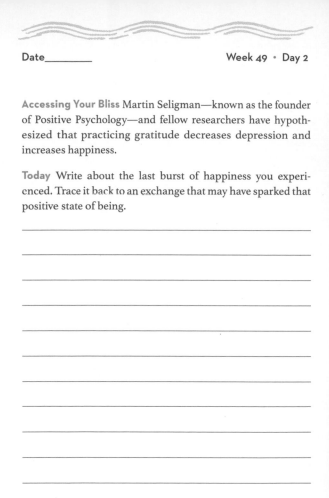

Accessing Your Bliss Martin Seligman—known as the founder of Positive Psychology—and fellow researchers have hypothesized that practicing gratitude decreases depression and increases happiness.

Today Write about the last burst of happiness you experienced. Trace it back to an exchange that may have sparked that positive state of being.

_____

_____

_____

_____

_____

_____

_____

_____

_____

_____

_____

_____

Leaving the Fast Lane Researchers at Northeastern University and Harvard University reported that subjects in their studies found that feelings of gratitude fostered greater patience, particularly when it came to financial matters.

Today Write about your current level of patience with your income and finances. No matter what that status may be, write at least one statement of gratitude for it, here.

_____

_____

_____

_____

_____

_____

_____

_____

_____

_____

_____

_____

Cultural Contributions Organizations that deliberately cult-
ivate a culture that promotes gratitude have found that
employees enjoy greater job satisfaction. Appreciation goes
a long way in the workplace.

Today Write about the culture in your current work environment. What aspect of it makes you feel happy, fulfilled, and
satisfied?

_____

_____

_____

_____

_____

_____

_____

_____

_____

_____

_____

_____

_____

Being Present

> *"The real gift of gratitude is that the more grateful*
> *you are, the more present you become."*

—Robert Holden, British psychologist, founder of the
Happiness Project, and author of *Happiness NOW!* and
Shift Happens!, among other best-selling books

Today Write about the last time you gave someone your complete and undivided attention. What did you learn about that person from the experience?

_____

_____

_____

_____

_____

_____

_____

_____

_____

_____

_____

Flipping the Influencer While Rebecca Solom's research has shown that cynicism, envy, indebtedness, and narcissism inhibit gratitude, she also acknowledges that other research shows that elevated states of gratitude inhibit those tendencies, which is fantastic! By now, I'm sure your own gratitude practice has reduced, if not eliminated, them.

Today Write about the positive impact your gratitude practice has had on lessening or actually doing away with any of your inclinations that could inhibit feelings of gratitude.

_____

_____

_____

_____

_____

_____

_____

_____

_____

_____

Using "Triggers" Jenny R. Craig, licensed clinical social worker, and inventor of the Grateful Ring™, suggests that there are two very important ways to deepen your experience as you engage in a gratitude practice:

> ✳ *It's best to perform your practice when your brain is most receptive, e.g., when you first wake up and just before going to sleep.*
>
> ✳ *A sensory event can also help trigger a grateful thought. Try a specific song or scent.*

Today Write about the ways you could enhance your gratitude practice. Do your best to access a sensory element that already has a positive effect on you.

_____

_____

_____

_____

_____

_____

_____

_____

Gratitude in Action #32 Making gratitude part of your family's credo creates an environment where everyone is uplifted. Modeling love and support through words and actions is a great way to raise your children. Writer and professional coach Emily Madill adds that it's not always an adult who steps up and takes the lead. Creating a meaningful ritual, such as a conversational round robin at the dinner table every evening or going on a hike together, gives each person in the family an opportunity to give thanks.

Today Write about a ritual you can set up with your family or your adopted family of friends.

_____

_____

_____

_____

_____

_____

_____

_____

_____

_____

Major Influencers Researchers have found that writing a letter to a person who has influenced you more than anyone else can increase your happiness level.

Today Write a letter to that person, below. How did the person influence you so strongly?

➤ Give yourself bonus points if you watch the SoulPancake video, "An Experiment in Gratitude," on YouTube—https://youtu.be/oHv6vTKD6lg—and make that phone call, too!

_____

_____

_____

_____

_____

_____

_____

_____

_____

_____

_____

_____

Toxic Words A study led by Joel Wong and Joshua Brown, both PhDs and professors of psychology at Indiana University, revealed insights into how written expressions of gratitude can improve mental health by shifting our emotions away from toxic emotions, like resentment and envy. When the researchers asked participants in the study to write gratitude letters, they discovered, to their surprise, that it was the lack of negative (toxic) emotion words, rather than an abundance of positive emotion words, that explained the writers' improved mental health.

Today Take a look at the writing you've done in this journal so far. Has your language changed over the past 49 weeks?

_____

_____

_____

_____

_____

_____

_____

_____

_____

_____

Satisfaction from a Distance The same study, referenced on Day 3 of this week, also showed that gratitude affects us positively, even if we don't share it directly with anyone else. Twenty-three percent of the gratitude letters written by the participants in the study were never sent, and yet the letter writers enjoyed mental health benefits nonetheless.

Today Write about a gratitude letter you'd like to send to someone, but have chosen not to, for whatever reason.

➤ **It's OK not to send that letter. Really.**

_____

_____

_____

_____

_____

_____

_____

_____

_____

_____

_____

Free Will versus Obligation If you believe that kindness is a choice, you're probably inclined to be more grateful to someone who has actually chosen to be kind, instead of feeling obligated to be kind. Neuroimaging backs this up. Researchers have found that the reward center of the brain lights up when a person perceives that a kindness was given freely, rather than out of obligation.

Today Write about an experience you've had with someone who was kind to you out of some sense of obligation. Consider how rewarding or meaningful—or not—it may have felt.

_____

_____

_____

_____

_____

_____

_____

_____

_____

_____

Mom was Right Gonzaga University published the first empirical evidence proving that expressing gratitude has a positive influence on how others perceive you. Professor Monica Y. Bartlett, who conducted the research at Gonzaga, said, "A simple thank-you leads people to view you as a warmer human being and, consequently, to be more interested in engaging with you socially and continuing to get to know you to build a relationship with you."

Today Write about how being thanked by a particular person led to a positive relationship.

_____

_____

_____

_____

_____

_____

_____

_____

_____

_____

Three Questions Keep it simple. The smallest contributions are often the most important ones.

- ✳ *What have you created for yourself and others?*
- ✳ *What unique mark are you making in the world?*
- ✳ *What are you truly grateful for?*

Today Write your responses below.

_____

_____

_____

_____

_____

_____

_____

_____

_____

_____

_____

_____

Gratitude in Action #33 Help someone else see their achievements and celebrate them. Life coach Chelsea Leigh Trescott suggests ending the day with a "ta-da" list rather than a "to do" list.

Today Write about someone you work with, are related to, or a friend who could use a little help recognizing their brilliance. Set a reminder on your phone to call that person and nudge the conversation toward a discussion of their "ta-da" list, based on what they achieved that day.

_____

_____

_____

_____

_____

_____

_____

_____

_____

_____

_____

_____

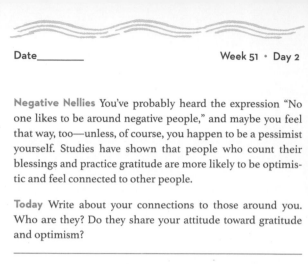

Negative Nellies You've probably heard the expression "No one likes to be around negative people," and maybe you feel that way, too—unless, of course, you happen to be a pessimist yourself. Studies have shown that people who count their blessings and practice gratitude are more likely to be optimistic and feel connected to other people.

Today Write about your connections to those around you. Who are they? Do they share your attitude toward gratitude and optimism?

Negative Detox Studies led by renowned gratitude researcher Robert A. Emmons, PhD, have shown that a daily gratitude practice has a beneficial effect on the mind and body by detoxifying negative thoughts and reducing stress.

Today Write a gratitude statement for a beautiful exchange you had with another person recently.

_____

_____

_____

_____

_____

_____

_____

_____

_____

_____

_____

_____

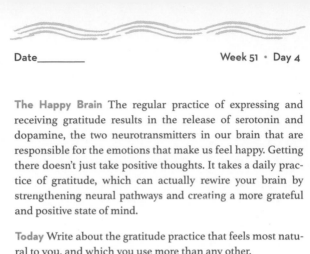

The Happy Brain The regular practice of expressing and receiving gratitude results in the release of serotonin and dopamine, the two neurotransmitters in our brain that are responsible for the emotions that make us feel happy. Getting there doesn't just take positive thoughts. It takes a daily practice of gratitude, which can actually rewire your brain by strengthening neural pathways and creating a more grateful and positive state of mind.

Today Write about the gratitude practice that feels most natural to you, and which you use more than any other.

_____

_____

_____

_____

_____

_____

_____

_____

_____

_____

Forging Onward Barbara De Angelis, personal growth advisor and spiritual teacher, encourages us not to abandon our practice of gratitude during challenging times, but to embrace it instead and understand that being grateful and unhappy or uncomfortable—all at the same time—are feelings that *can* coexist. In fact, you need your gratitude practice more than ever in times of discomfort and pain.

Today Write about the one thing you can be grateful for, no matter how rough life gets.

_____

_____

_____

_____

_____

_____

_____

_____

_____

_____

_____

Bus Magic Taking a shuttle bus on the way home from the airport, after a week spent at Walt Disney World, Cass McCrory, a marketing strategist, business podcaster, and mother of four, asked her daughter, "What was your favorite part of the trip?" Secretly, Cass was hoping for a reply that might reflect her daughter's gratitude for the experience. Instead, her daughter said, "I love the bus rides!" The magical and amazing thing about young children is that they are able to be in the moment and feel grateful for exactly what is happening in *the now*.

Today Be here now, in this very moment. Look up, then write a statement of gratitude for something that's right in front of you.

_____

_____

_____

_____

_____

_____

_____

_____

_____

_____

Ditch the Drama The way to a grateful life is not to take it so seriously or allow yourself to get so wrapped up in daily dramas that you miss out on the beauty of everything around you. Block out the things that needlessly distract you.

Today Write about a single, simple, beautiful element in your environment that you would have missed if you allowed yourself to get distracted by needless drama.

_____

_____

_____

_____

_____

_____

_____

_____

_____

_____

_____

_____

Gratitude and Joy

> *"In my 12 years of research on 11,000 pieces of data,*
> *I did not interview one person who had described*
> *themselves as joyful, who also did not actively practice*
> *gratitude. For me it was very counterintuitive because*
> *I went into the research thinking that the relationship*
> *between joy and gratitude was: if you are joyful,*
> *you should be grateful. But it wasn't that way at all.*
> *Instead, practicing gratitude invites joy into our lives."*

—Brené Brown, research professor for the University of Houston and best-selling author of *The Gifts of Imperfection*, *Daring Greatly*, *Rising Strong*, *Braving the Wilderness*, and *Dare to Lead*

Today Write about the aspects of your gratitude journal practice that have resonated the most with you. What part would you like to continue to use in your ongoing gratitude practice?

_____

_____

_____

_____

_____

_____

_____

_____

Intention 2.0 Setting an intention is like using a beacon to tell the world who you want to be, and how you want to influence others and engage with people around you. Setting an intention puts the focus on the positive and serves as a reminder of how you want to live each day.

Today Consider the intention entries you've written in this journal in previous weeks. Some may have resonated with you more than others. Write an all-encompassing intention statement that you can use as your daily mantra from now on.

➤ **Keep it short and sweet.**

_____

_____

_____

_____

_____

_____

_____

_____

_____

Practice Method You can choose to practice gratitude any way you like, whether you continue to keep a journal, use a gratitude jar, or keep on your smartphone a running list of things for which you are grateful. No matter which method you choose, just be sure to do it daily so that practicing gratitude becomes an automatic habit.

Today In the space below, write about the method you've chosen for your practice and any tools you might use in that practice.

➤ Your brain is most receptive when you first wake up or just before you go to sleep.

_____

_____

_____

_____

_____

_____

_____

_____

_____

Default Method Let's face it: Life gets busy and some days can be insane! It's important to have a backup plan for those days to help you maintain consistency in your gratitude practice. Doing this is no different than keeping an emergency snack in your purse or backpack.

Today Write about what your gratitude practice backup plan might be.

➤ The A, B, C method from Week 36-Day 2 is an easy one to follow. If you have a smartphone, chances are you'll never be without a backup; it will literally be in the palm of your hand.

_____

_____

_____

_____

_____

_____

_____

_____

_____

Cornerstone GIAs The gratitude in action practice you've engaged in is a critical part of the cycle of giving and receiving. GIAs are deliberate acts of kindness, thoughtfulness, or help that you offer to others. A GIA is not necessarily about giving material things or writing thank-you notes, although those expressions are perfectly fine. The idea is to choose GIAs that resonate with you and then make them part of your practice.

Today Write about the types of GIAs that you will continue to do, as a part of your practice. List three to five ideas below.

_____

_____

_____

_____

_____

_____

_____

_____

_____

_____

_____

Buddy Up Ask someone to be your gratitude buddy and accountability partner. You might consider using this journal as a way to guide you through a daily practice together.

Today Consider who might be a good buddy for you. Write about that person and why they could be a good fit. If you have a small group of friends with whom you'd like to buddy up, even better!

_____

_____

_____

_____

_____

_____

_____

_____

_____

_____

_____

_____

Ancestry

"For sound evolutionary reasons, most of us are not nearly as good at dwelling on good events as we are at analyzing bad events. Those of our ancestors who spent a lot of time basking in the sunshine of good events, when they should have been preparing for disaster, did not survive the Ice Age. So to overcome our brains' natural catastrophic bent, we need to work on and practice this skill of thinking about what went well."

—Martin Seligman, PhD, American psychologist and author, commonly known as the founder of Positive Psychology

Today Write about three good things that happened to you this week.

_____

_____

_____

_____

_____

_____

_____

_____

Your Gratitude Practice Road Map

Using the road map below, fill in the elements that will make up your new gratitude practice. Refer to Week 52 for prompts to help you customize your plan.

My daily intention:

_____

_____

_____

My gratitude practice tools:

_____

_____

_____

On days that are hectic, my default gratitude practice tool will be:

_____

_____

_____

The cornerstone GIAs I will implement as often as possible are:

_____

_____

_____

Contributors

Sara B. Algoe received her PhD in social psychology from the University of Virginia. She is an assistant professor of psychology and neuroscience and the director of (EASIR) Laboratory at the University of North Carolina at Chapel Hill.

Summer Allen is a graduate of Carleton College and Brown University. She is a research/writing fellow with the Greater Good Science Center at the University of California–Berkeley, authoring several research papers, including "The Science of Gratitude." She also writes a blog for the American Association for the Advancement of Science.

Maya Angelou (1928–2014) was an American poet, singer, author, and civil rights activist.

Monica Y. Bartlett received her master's degree in criminal justice from Northeastern University in Boston. Further connecting antisocial behavior to crime prompted her to earn a doctorate in social psychology. She is an associate professor and chair of the Psychology Department at Gonzaga University, focusing on the positive effects of gratitude on our relationships.

Melody Beattie is a Minnesota-born self-help author and authority on addiction and recovery circles. She has written 15 books, including the international best seller *Codependent No More*.

Henry Ward Beecher (1813–1887) was a clergyman, social reformer, and speaker, best known for supporting the abolition of slavery. He acquired fame for his novel oratorical style, integrating humor, dialect, and slang.

Thanissaro Bhikkhu is abbot of the Metta Forest Monastery in San Diego County, California. He is the author of *Wings to Awakening* and *Mind Like Fire Unbound*.

Ali Binazir is a "happiness engineer," coach, speaker, and author who graduated from Harvard College, the University of California–San Diego School of Medicine, and Cambridge University.

Joan Borysenko is president of Mind/Body Health Sciences Inc. She is a cancer cell biologist, a licensed psychologist, and the author of five books, including *The Power of the Mind to Heal* and *Minding the Body, Mending the Mind*.

Carolyn A. Bratton is an ordained minister and the cofounder of Lifestream Center in Roanoke, Virginia.

Loretta Graziano Breuning is the author of *Habits of a Happy Brain* and professor emerita of management at California State University–East Bay.

Brené Brown is an American research professor at the University of Houston. She has spent the last two decades studying shame, vulnerability, and empathy, and authoring books and coaching programs on these topics.

Joshua Brown, PhD, is a professor of psychology at Indiana University.

The Buddha (also known as Siddhartha Gotama or Siddhārtha Gautama), who lived in the fifth through the fourth century BCE, was a philosopher, spiritual teacher, and religious leader.

Carol Bush is the impact and innovation director of Susan B. Komen "Race for the Cure" Kansas & Western Missouri. She is also an oncology nurse activist, social entrepreneur, podcast host, and health-care social media influencer.

Julia Cameron is an artist, poet, playwright, filmmaker, and the author of *The Artist Way, Vein of Gold*, and *Blessings, among other books.*

David W. Chan is professor in the Department of Educational Psychology at the Chinese University of Hong Kong in Hong Kong.

Yoichi Chida is a professor of Positive Psychology, faculty of human happiness, at the Happy Science University in Japan. He is an expert in the mind-body-spirit connection and the intersection of religion and health.

Deepak Chopra is an internationally known expert in the field of alternative medicine. He is the founder of the Chopra Center and has written a number of best-selling books, including *Metahuman: Unleashing Your Infinite Potential* and *The 7 Spiritual Laws of Success.*

Nicholas Christakis is a physician and sociologist. He is a professor of social and natural science at Yale University, with areas of interest that include network science, health, medicine, and biosocial science.

Jenny R. Craig is a board-certified diplomate clinical social worker, an innovator in brain-training tools, a leadership coach, a team builder and speaker, and the best-selling author of *Talking Tips and Healing Tools for Trauma: Helping Children After a Trauma* and *Grace and Bella: The Forgiving Heart.* Craig is also the founder of the Grateful Ring™ movement.

His Holiness the 14th Dalai Lama is the spiritual leader of Tibet.

Mary Anne Davis is an Irish social entrepreneur, activist, and champion for the rights and inclusion of children and adults with intellectual disabilities. She has been the chief executive officer of Special Olympics International since May 2016.

Barbara De Angelis is a teacher in the field of personal and spiritual development. She has written 16 best-selling books, including *Chicken Soup for the Couple's Soul* and *How Did I Get Here? Finding Your Way to Renewed Hope and Happiness When Life and Love Take Unexpected Turns.*

David DeSteno earned his PhD at Yale University and is a professor of psychology at Northeastern University. The author of *Emotional Success: The Power of Gratitude, Compassion, and Pride,* he is a fellow of the American Psychological Association and the Association for Psychological Science, as well as the editor in chief of the American Psychological Association's journal *Emotion.*

Fred De Witt Van Amburgh is the author of *By the Side of the Road, Just Common Sense,* and *The Mental Spark Plug.*

Meerabelle Dey has earned a BA in history and religious studies from the University of Toronto and a JD from the Fordham University School of Law.

Leah Dickens is a psychologist specializing in social perception, nonverbal behaviors, and the functions of emotions in everyday life, such as pride, gratitude, and how these can be beneficial to the self and relationships. She is an assistant professor at Kenyon College in Gambier, Ohio.

Mike Dooley is a *New York Times* best-selling author of *A Beginner's Guide to the Universe*, *Infinite Possibilities*, and *Life on Earth*; metaphysical teacher; cofounder of Tut.com (The Universe Talks); and creator of "Notes from the Universe."

Albert Einstein (1879–1955) was a German-born theoretical physicist who developed the theory of relativity, one of the two pillars of modern physics. His work is also known for its influence on the philosophy of science.

Robert A. Emmons, PhD, is an American psychologist and professor at University of California–Davis. He is an expert in the field of personality psychology, emotion psychology, and the psychology of religion. Emmons's research focuses on the psychology of gratitude and the psychology of individual goal setting.

Robert Enright is a psychologist and professor at the University of Wisconsin–Madison. Considered "the forgiveness trailblazer" by *Time* magazine, he has written over 150 publications and seven books, and lectures internationally on forgiveness therapy and forgiveness education.

Laura Federico, LCSW, specializes in self-worth concerns, self-empowerment, and the mind-body connection.

Piero Ferrucci is a psychotherapist, philosopher, and the author of *The Power of Kindness*, *What We May Be*, *Inevitable Grace*, and *What Our Children Teach Us*; he coauthored *The Child of Your Dreams*. He is also a staff member of the Psychosynthesis Institute of Florence, Italy, and the International Federation of Medical Psychotherapy.

Melanie K. Finney teaches in the Department of Communication and Theatre at DePauw University. She focuses on the social construction of personal and social identities, intercultural communications, gender, race, class, and culture.

Zoketsu Norman Fischer holds an MFA from the University of Iowa Writer's Workshop and a master's from the Graduate Theological Union at the University of California–Berkeley. Fisher is a writer, poet, and author of more than 16 books. He has been a Zen Buddhist priest and abbot for the San Francisco Zen Center.

Robert H. Frank received his bachelor's degree in mathematics from Georgia Tech, and a master's in statistics and a PhD in economics from the University of California–Berkeley. Currently he is professor of economics at Cornell's Johnson Graduate School of Management. For more than a decade, he has written the "Economic View" column for the *New York Times*.

Barbara L. Fredrickson is a Kenan distinguished professor of psychology and principal investigator of Positive Emotions and Psychophysiology Lab (PEPLab) at the University of North Carolina at Chapel Hill. Her area of focus is emotions and Positive Psychology. She has written the books *Positivity: Top-Notch Research Reveals the 3-to-1 Ratio That Will Change Your Life* and *Love 2.0*.

Philip Friedman is a licensed psychologist and creator of the Friedman Assessment Scales on Well-Being, Beliefs, Quality of Life, Affect, Life Balance, Spiritual Awakening and the Mini-5 Factor Personality Scale. He is also the developer of the ICBEST model of psychotherapy. Friedman is the author of *The Forgiveness Solution* and *Creating Well-Being*.

Ross Gay is an American poet with a master's from Sarah Lawrence College and a doctorate in American literature from Temple University. He has authored *Against Which*, *Bringing the Shovel Down*, and *Catalog of Unabashed Gratitude*, as well as a collection of essays, titled *The Book of Delights*.

Thomas Gilovich is a professor of psychology at Cornell University. His research focuses on everyday human judgment, social psychology, decision making, and behavioral economics, and he has written several books, including *The Wisest One in the Room: How You Can Benefit from Social Psychology's Most Powerful Insights*.

Francesca Gino is a professor of business administration in the Negotiation, Organizations & Markets Unit at Harvard Business School. She is affiliated with the Program on Negotiations at Harvard Law School and the Behavioral Insights Group at Harvard's Kennedy School. She's authored *Rebel Talent: Why It Pays to Break the Rules in Work and Life*.

Richelle E. Goodrich is a writer, poet, and essayist. She has earned bachelor's degrees in liberal arts studies and math/natural sciences education from Eastern Washington University.

Adam Grant has been rated Wharton's top professor for seven years in a row. He is an organizational psychologist, podcaster, and a TEDx speaker specializing in motivation and meaning, and living more generous and creative lives. Grant is a four-time *New York Times* best-selling author of books such as *Give and Take*, *Originals*, and *Option B*.

Robert Holden is a British psychologist and the founder of the Happiness Project. Holden works in the field of Positive Psychology and well-being, and is considered Britain's foremost authority on happiness. He is the author of *Happiness NOW!* and *Shift Happens!*, among other best-selling books.

David Hume is an 18th-century Scottish historian, philosopher, and economist.

Andrea Hussong is a developmental scientist and licensed clinical psychologist, focusing on substance abuse and the development of children of drug-involved parents. She is the director of the Carolina Consortium on Human Development in North Carolina.

Christina Karns is a research associate in psychology at the University of Oregon and the Center for Brain Injury Research and Training, and director of the Emotions and Neuroplasticity Project at the University of Oregon.

Todd B. Kashdan is a renowned expert on well-being, social relationships, stress, and anxiety. He has published more than 185 articles in scientific journals, which have been translated into 15 different languages. Dr. Kashdan is a professor of psychology and a senior scientist at the Center for the Advancement of Well-Being at George Mason University.

John F. Kennedy was the 35th president of the United States.

Jack Kornfield is a Buddhist-trained monk who has taught meditation since 1974 and holds a doctorate in clinical psychology. He is the founder of the Meditation Society in Barre, Massachusetts.

Neal Krause is a Marshall H. Becker collegiate professor of public health at the University of Michigan School of Public Health, in Ann Arbor, Michigan, focusing on stress and the resources people use to cope with it.

Sonja Lyubomirsky is a professor of psychology at the University of California–Riverside and the author of the best-selling books *The How of Happiness* and *The Myths of Happiness*.

Emily Madill is a certified professional coach, writer, and editor-at-large for *Thrive Global*, the world's first behavior change platform.

Michael "Tender Heart" Markley is the chairperson of the Seaconke-Wamapnoag tribe in southern Massachusetts.

Angie Mattson Stegall is a life and business coach and the award-winning author of five books, including *Make Some Room: Powerful Life Lessons Inspired by an Epic 16-Day Colorado River Rafting Trip through Grand Canyon* and *Ponder This: How Everyday Experiences Deliver Unexpected Insights in Business and Life.*

Cass McCrory is the founding marketing strategist at Capra Strategy, host of the Real Women in Business podcast, and the mother of four.

Maureen McCullough is the Northeast/Mid-Atlantic regional field director of Catholic Relief Services.

Michael E. McCullough is a professor of psychology at the University of Miami and director of the Laboratory for Social and Clinical Psychology. He is the author of *Beyond Revenge: The Evolution of the Forgiveness Instinct.*

Mother Teresa (born Mary Teresa Bojaxhiu) was an honored Roman Catholic nun and missionary. In 1950, she founded the Missionaries of Charity, which manages homes for those dying of HIV/AIDS, leprosy, and tuberculosis; runs soup kitchens; and supports the poorest of the poor through various other programs.

Caroline Myss is an expert in the fields of human consciousness, spirituality, energy medicine, and the science of medical intuition. She is a five-time *New York Times* best-selling author and international speaker. Her book credits include *Invisible Acts of Power, Anatomy of the Spirit*, and *Sacred Contracts.*

Daniel T. Peralta is a teacher of metaphysics, holding a degree in the psychology of consciousness from Antioch University.

Paul W. Pruyser (1916–1987) was a clinical psychologist and writer who contributed to the psychology or religion field in his work with the Menninger Clinic, now located in Houston, Texas.

Margaret Rutherford is a psychologist, blogger, podcaster, and the author of *Perfectly Hidden Depression: How to Break Free from the Perfectionism that Masks Your Depression.* Additionally, she has written for the *Huffington Post*, Psych Central, and the Good Men Project.

Anne Wilson Schaef is a feminist and psychotherapist. She is an internationally known author, speaker, consultant, and seminar leader, and has written 16 internationally best-selling books, including *When Society Becomes an Addict* and *Meditations for Women Who Do Too Much.*

Martin Seligman is an American psychologist, known as the founder of the Positive Psychology movement. He is the author of self-help books on resilience, learned helplessness, depression, optimism, and pessimism. Seligman is also a recognized authority on interventions that prevent depression and build strength and well-being.

Chrys Sills is an enterprise transformation delivery consultant with a degree in industrial/organizational psychology from Purdue University. She fosters joy in her life through her creative approach to knitting.

Georg Simmel (1858–1918) was a lecturer at the University of Berlin, an author, and part of the first generation of German sociologists who pioneered new analyses of social individuality, fragmentation, urban life, and the form of the metropolis. Simmel's most famous works today are *The Problems of the Philosophy of History, The Philosophy of Money, The Metropolis*, and *Mental Life*.

Adam Smith (1723–1790) was a Scottish economist, philosopher, author, and pioneer of political economy. He is best known as the "Father of Economics" or the "Father of Capitalism." Smith wrote two classic works, *The Theory of Moral Sentiments* and *An Inquiry into the Nature and Causes of the Wealth of Nations*.

Rebecca C. Solom, MS, LCMHC, is a clinical psychologist and the author of *Thieves of Thankfulness: Inhibitors of Gratitude*.

David Steindl-Rast is a Benedictine monk, lecturer, and the author of *Gratefulness, The Heart of Prayer*. Brother David is a catalyst for interfaith dialogue and has worked to more closely integrate spirituality and science. He also holds a PhD in experimental psychology.

Andrew D. Steptoe is a professor of psychology and director of the Research Department of Behaviour Science and Health at the Faculty of Population Health Sciences at the University College London, UK.

Samantha Sutton is a life engineer, and a career and executive coach. She earned a PhD is science and engineering from MIT.

Marla Tabaka is a small-business advisor, who helps entrepreneurs around the globe grow their businesses. She has more than 25 years of experience in corporate and start-up ventures and speaks widely on combining strategic and creative thinking. She is also a regular columnist for Inc.com.

Karl-Halvor Teigen is a psychologist and professor emeritus of psychology at the University of Norway. His most significant contributions are in the study of assessment and decision-making processes. He has published numerous articles in international psychology journals and contributed to several books.

Loren Toussaint is a professor of psychology at Luther College. His area of research is on how forgiveness affects our mental and physical health. He has served as a consultant to the Mayo Clinic and Cancer Treatment Centers of America.

Chelsea Leigh Trescott is a certified life coach, breakup specialist, advice columnist, and podcast host of *"Thank You Heartbreak."*